Culture Impact

Strategies to Create World-Changing Workplaces

Melanie Booher

Lina Clavijo

Kirstie Dierig

Tosca DiMatteo

Rita Ernst

Elisabeth Galperin

Tiersa Hall

Karen Hewitt

Susan LePlae Miller

Angie Redmon

Melanie Rodriguez

Doug Whitney

Contents

Introduction   1

1. Beyond the Logo   5

    Doug Whitney   21

2. Intentional Culture Creation   23

    Karen Hewitt   49

3. Becoming an Award-Winning Workplace   51

    Angie Redmon   75

4. HR's Role in Company Culture   79

    Kristie Dierig   97

5. Gamifying Culture   101

    Melanie Booher   123

6. Inner Critics   125

    Tosca DiMatteo   151

7. Impact Through Inclusion   153

    Melanie Rodriguez   169

8. Culture Repair   171

    Rita Ernst   195

9. Team Impact   197

    Susan LePlae Miller   215

10. Impactful Leadership   219

     Tiersa Hall   243

11. Culture Matters   247

     Elisabeth Galperin   265

12. Curiosity at the Heart of Inclusion   267

     Lina Clavijo   279

     Conclusion   281

     About Influence Network Media   285

     Book Smarts Business Podcast   287

Introduction

Workplace culture is the personality of an organization. It's the shared beliefs, values, and attitudes that shape the way people interact with each other and with their work. A strong workplace culture can be a powerful asset for an organization, helping to attract and retain top talent, boost productivity, and improve customer satisfaction.

In *Culture Impact*, we'll explore the best practices and strategies for creating a world-changing workplace culture. Covered in this book you will find defining company values to gamifying your culture to make that culture memorable, meaningful, and pervasive. Stories are shared from leaders that have successfully created world-changing cultures.

Sharing and learning from others is important – and knowing when to utilize others' expertise to help move our business forward is just as important. That's the beauty of this collective.

We've pulled together a stellar group of leaders to collaborate and create *Culture Impact: Strategies to Create World-changing Workplaces*. These authors' amazing chapters are a culmination of shared expertise related to their years of experience and highly honed craft. Years of ongoing learning, trying new methods, advancing new technologies, and serving clients are all collected here within these pages. Read and internalize their words. Learn from them. Decide which pieces of their guidance make the most sense to improve your organization, then strategize and move forward.

By the end of this book, you'll have the tools and knowledge you need to create a workplace culture that inspires your employees, drives innovation, and helps you achieve your organization's goals.

It's important to note, this book is not meant to be all-encompassing story with every aspect covered related to workplace culture – we don't have enough pages for that! However, if you are seeking some fresh perspective from leaders who have driven culture success (both for themselves and others!) then this book is for you. Or maybe you are looking for new ideas to improve processes, develop your team, or guide your organization into the 21st century? *Culture Impact* will get you thinking outside the box and geared to try new things within your organization.

Each chapter can certainly be read as an independent short story written by an expert in their field. These experts, our wonderful authors, offer ideas to raise the bar of your existing efforts. We encourage you to find golden nuggets within these pages to expand where you already have the knowledge, to challenge the "that's how we've always done it" mindset, and to delve into different realms as you try something new.

If the essential business areas presented within *Culture Impact* inspire you but leave you wanting more or in need of more help to get your needs/wants accomplished, then we encourage you to reach out to our thought leaders for additional help, accountability, coaching, and/or consulting. Definitely connect with them on LinkedIn (their LinkedIn accounts can be found at the end of their bios) – just knowing them will help level up your game.

We believe this book will provide you with a myriad of innovative ideas to drive your workplace culture forward in a positive and effective way. By following the guidance provided in *Culture Impact: Strategies to Create World-changing Workplaces*, you can create a world-changing workplace culture that inspires your employees, drives innovation, and helps you achieve your organization's goals.

Don't be afraid to think differently – that's how progress is made. Think outside the box and try new things. Join us on a journey as we explore how amazing *Culture Impact* strategies can impact your life and workplace culture in new and exciting ways.

~ Melanie Booher, PEOPLEfirst & INM President

I.

Beyond the Logo

Exploring the Influence of Brand Perception on Company Culture

Doug Whitney | Experienced Leader, Brand Marketer, Strategist

> *"It takes twenty years to build a reputation and five minutes to ruin it. If you think about that, you'll do things differently." – Warren Buffett*

Introduction:

When we think about brand perception, we typically think about how customers perceive our brand. However, I'd like to explore an underappreciated side of brand perception – how do your employees perceive your brand? And why does it matter when it comes to company culture?

First – let's define brand perception. Brand perception refers to the subjective impressions, beliefs, opinions, and feelings that individuals or groups hold about a brand. In short – it's equivalent to an individual's personality. Just as we relate to other people based on their actions, words, appearance, and preferences – we do the same thing with brands (whether you realize it or not, it's happening).

Now, let's frame up company culture. A company's culture is the shared values, beliefs, norms, traditions, behaviors, and practices. These shape the overall working environment, attitudes, and behaviors of employees within an organization. This is where it starts to get *very* interesting.

Let's key in on the last two pieces of that definition: **attitudes** and **behaviors**. As a leader or business owner, do you want your employees to come into work with a negative attitude each day? As a leader or business owner, do you want employees expressing behavior that is detrimental to the business? **This** is why culture is so extremely important, and why folks like me (and the other authors of this book) care about it so deeply. The reasoning and thesis on this is simple:

> *Performance is directly correlated to culture.*

If employees have a poor perception of your brand, the culture will suffer. If the culture suffers, so does performance. When performance suffers, the business fails. It's that simple.

What is brand perception?

Brand perception is formed over time, and across mediums. It is the culmination of the following:

- Image: Comprised of visual elements (logo, design, colors, etc.)
- Messaging: The words you use to describe your brand and any formal communication (press releases, social media, internal newsletters, etc.)
- Reputation: Product quality, customer service
- Associations: The company you keep (sponsorships, partnerships) – stances on social issues also reside here

Again, just as we are constantly forming perceptions about individuals based on our experiences with them – we do the same with brands every day. We form opinions based on what we see, hear, and feel.

For employees of the brand – this is particularly important, but often overlooked. Let's circle back to those two keywords we highlighted earlier – **attitude** and **behavior**. Employees are picking up signals all day, every day. From every micro-interaction to major announcements, every ad placement, every piece of content, and every team meeting – signals are being sent and received. Great brands and leaders understand this, and as a result, **send signals that** *encourage the types of attitudes and behaviors they want to see*. Not only does this encourage these attitudes and behaviors from current employees, but it also attracts potential talent who embody those same attributes. This is how brand perception shapes company culture.

However – and this is important – the inverse is also true. If employees have a negative experience working for a company, what perception do you think begins to form? If leadership consistently misses the mark with internal communications, partners with companies who have shady business practices, and promotes leaders who provide poor customer service to their direct reports (yes, leadership is a "service" when done correctly – but that's a topic for another day) – how do you think employees will behave and talk about the brand? Do you think they'll be giving their best effort? Word travels fast in a small town, and thanks to technology and the emergence of social platforms, the world is now smaller than ever. If your employees have a poor perception of your brand, it will be known. Both by your customers, and potential talent.

The Business Case

At this point, I can hear you saying, "Ok, ok, I get it – I should care how employees feel about my brand. But does this **actually** affect the bottom line?" Let's talk about that.

In a 2019 report published by SHRM (Society for Human Resource Management), their research showed that 1-in-5 Americans left their organizations due to bad company culture over a five-year period. The associated cost of that turnover? A mind-boggling $223 billion (that's billion, with a B). Yikes! [1]

Though they don't share the line items that comprise this massive total in the report, we can deduce a few things with a bit of business acumen. Most obviously: recruiting is incredibly expensive. The harder it is for your recruiter to find willing talent, the more expensive it becomes. This is easy math. If you have a desirable brand that people are clambering to work for, the recruiter gets to focus on sifting through an abundance of candidates to find the best talent. If your brand is not desirable, your recruiter is likely not going to have the luxury of many candidates to choose from, and will instead have to spend time *pursuing* candidates – which takes much longer and involves a **sales process** to even receive a resumé! I'll reiterate here – easy math. You can either start with resumés and select the best ones, or have to search and plead for people to submit them. If your brand perception is poor, the talent will not only be worse, it will also be more expensive.

Not only do you have to pay the recruiter to find talent, but you (and others from the hiring manager, director, and other teammates who may be involved in the recruiting process) also spend hours upon hours of valuable time searching for talent. Today's interview processes are more bloated than ever – often requiring three to five rounds of interviews with a total of four to seven employees participating. Let's assume we have an hour-long interview for five employees at an average salary of $150k, with five candidates for a single role. Frankly, it's more likely this is happening for eight to ten candidates for a single role, but I'll be conservative. The total cost for **hosting the interviews** alone is nearly $2,000. This doesn't factor in interview prep, coordinating the interviews, paying the recruiter's salary, loss of output from the interviewer's negotiations...should I go on? You get it.

Another key line item in this $223 billion is the cost of training, onboarding, and loss of output. Generally speaking, it takes around thirty-six days to replace an existing employee, about six months for the new employee to get onboarded, trained, and producing at a reasonable level, and twelve to eighteen months to reach the productivity of an existing employee. That's thirty-six days of **zero** output, six months of ~50% output, and another six to twelve months of 75% output, before finally reaching full productivity. **Expensive**.

It goes without saying that this loss of output has other consequences. Growth may slow down due to the reduced output. All too often, however, more pressure is placed on other existing employees to "pick up the slack" which eventually leads to burnout and more turnover further leading to poor morale and **even more** turnover. This snowball can be devastating to a company's culture, and once it obtains a certain level of momentum it is incredibly difficult to stem the bleeding.

Lastly, and excitingly, the companies at the apex of brand perception enjoy a unique and valuable perk – employees are often willing to take a **discount** to work there. For example, a 2019 survey from "Fast Company" highlighted that nearly half of all respondents (and 75% of millennials!) said they'd be willing to take a $5,000 – $10,000 pay cut to work for a company that's environmentally responsible.[2] Values create value.

Dieselgate: A Costly Lesson

Leading up to 2015, Volkswagen (VW) – a leading German automobile manufacturer – had positioned themselves as an environmentally responsible brand, promoting their diesel vehicles as "clean diesel" and emphasizing their commitment to sustainability and low emissions. They had invested heavily in marketing and advertising campaigns that portrayed their diesel vehicles as "eco-friendly" and in compliance with emissions regulations. However, it was discovered in 2015 that they had installed software in their diesel vehicles to **cheat** on emissions tests, allowing their vehicles to emit more pollutants than what was reported to regulators – and the public.

Trust in VW was eroded immediately. Consumers, activists,

and shareholders were furious. The backlash was swift and unforgiving – in the United States alone VW had to reach a settlement with the FTC and EPA to the tune of **$14.7 billion;** which included having to buy back vehicles from customers who had been duped by VW's falsities. It would take years to regain consumer trust and has weighed heavily on the VW brand since.

This hit to brand perception injured the company culture as well. We can imagine how many employees likely felt: embarrassed, betrayed, disillusioned, and demoralized. The financial impact also led to workforce reductions, restructuring efforts, and other cost-cutting measures. The trust of VW employees had been battered and would take years to recover through various initiatives.

What we can learn from Dieselgate is the **_number one rule_** of building both a positive brand perception and a strong culture: your actions must, **must**, match your words.

Patagonia: Authenticity Rules

On the opposite end of the spectrum, we have Patagonia. Genuinely, I cannot think of a company that lives its values more fervently than these folks.

Patagonia's mission, as stated on their website, is: "We're in business to save our home planet."[3] Immediately, you start to form the perception that they care about the environment. But do their actions match their words?

Hold onto your seat.

For nearly thirty years they've donated 1% of their sales to preservation efforts – equating to over $140 million. They're a certified B-corp. 100% of the electricity in their US facilities comes from renewable resources. They provide time off for employees to engage in (peaceful) environmental activism – and get this – they'll even pay your bail if protests turn not-so-peaceful.

More recently, however, they kicked it up a notch. In a public letter from founder Yvon Chouinard, he announced that he was donating the entire company. Yes, you read that correctly. 100% of the voting stock would be put into a Trust created to protect the company's values, and 100% of the non-voting stock was donated to a non-profit dedicated to fighting the environmental crisis and defending nature. A billionaire donated his entire company to the cause, and added an exclamation point with this epic tagline, "As of now, Earth is our only shareholder."[4] Now **that** is putting your money where your mouth is.

Oh, by the way, it turns out they care about the humans on Earth, too. In addition to generous health insurance, maternity **and** paternity leave (as well another top-end benefits) they also offer more unique perks like: on-site childcare for working parents, workout classes, multiple organic cafés, and if you're a working parent traveling for work, they'll even pay to send a nanny with you.

The payoff? Immense.

Patagonia has a turnover rate of just 4%, which is less than a third of the industry-average 13%. A mind-boggling 100% of mothers return to work after maternity leave.[5] While a Gallup poll in 2022 reported that a meager 21% of respondents (across all industries and companies) felt engaged at work, over 90% of Patagonia's employees report that they are proud to work for Patagonia and believe the company has a bright future.[6] Patagonia also scored extremely high marks from employees on the company living its core values, fulfilling its mission statement, and employees feeling that their immediate manager/ supervisor cares about their well-being – the list goes on.

Oh, they've also grown from $3 million in revenue to over $1 billion.

This is the power of authenticity. You may not agree with or be excited by Patagonia's values, but you can't deny their impact. You can't poke holes in their actions. If you buy their products, you don't question where the money is going. They walk the talk, and their employees follow suit.

Managing Brand Perception and Company Culture

So, how do we align our desired brand perception and our company culture?

Unsurprisingly, it starts with purpose. Why do you exist? By understanding why you exist, customers and employees alike get the opportunity to find out if their values align with yours. If you haven't already seen Simon Sinek's viral "Start With Why" TED Talk, go ahead and bookmark this page right now and go watch it. [7]

Once you have your "**why**," you can then create your values. Here's the key:

Every company has values. Good companies have the **right** values. **Great** companies **live** those values.

Your values should act as guiding principles to accomplish your purpose. If your purpose is a North Star, your values act as the compass to guide that journey. More importantly, they should act as a decision-making litmus test for anyone in the company. If a decision would pass the "Values Litmus Test," then it's a good decision. If it doesn't, it's a bad decision. This may sound over-simplified, but when your values are clear, enforced, and displayed by leadership it can be extremely powerful and highly efficient.

I could dedicate an entire chapter to the process of creating values, but here are the three keys to getting started:

1. **Avoid generalities, avoid commonalities**. Nearly every company highlights "integrity" and "teamwork/collaboration." While these are great values, they've become so overused by companies who don't uphold those values that they've lost their meaning. To combat this, be specific. What does integrity mean *for us*? What does teamwork/collaboration mean *for us*? Defining these values gives employees greater context and clues on what behaviors they should exhibit.

2. **Don't mistake finite goals for long-term values**. Listen, I've heard "winning" and "excellence" mentioned by CEOs more than I care to mention. Sure, winning is great but what does that mean, really? The goal of "winning" works for sports teams who are all competing for one championship, because it's a finite game. There is a clearly defined set of rules, a clear winner, and a clear loser. Unlike sports, business is an infinite "game." There are no clearly defined rules, and not all participants are even aware that they are "playing the game." The game has no clear beginning, nor does it have a defined ending. So, logically, no one can ever be crowned "the winner." In fact, there may be multiple people winning – and some losing – all at the same time. So, what exactly are you chasing? I'm not suggesting you shouldn't try to lead your field – but in an infinite game the goal should not be to lead at any given point.

It should be to perpetuate the game and lead it for as long as possible. In order to do this, you must set values accordingly.

3. **Be authentic**. This is, by far, the most important aspect. As we showcased earlier, the quickest way to damage your brand (and your culture) is misalignment of words and actions. Do not create "lip service" values that you aren't prepared to relentlessly act upon. This is where many companies falter, even if well-intentioned. If "integrity" is a core value, then enforce it relentlessly, not just when it is convenient to do so. The more authentic your values, the more your employees (and customers) will connect with them. Over time, this will lead to higher engagement, higher performance, lower turnover, and – crucially – an excellent work environment.

Establishing your "*why*" and core values are a great start – but they are only the beginning. These words **must** guide your actions. Establishing employee training, recognition programs, incentive programs, and ongoing brand marketing campaigns are just a few tactical actions that you can (and should) take to build the culture you wish to see. Set periodic check-ins to evaluate whether or not you're keeping your word. It takes extraordinary commitment to uphold, but if your values and purpose are *authentic*, it will be easier than you expect. Be vigilant.

Closing Thoughts

If the road to hell is paved with good intentions, then the road to positive culture is paved with authentic actions. Be who you say you are; do what you say you're going to do. By doing so, an **accurate** and **sustainable** perception is created – allowing customers and employees alike to align their values accordingly. Will you win every sale? No. Will you attract **all** the top talent? Also no. You **will** increase your odds of achieving both. By aligning on **values**, you grease the wheels for transactions to take place. You may lose out on some transactions that you likely weren't going to win anyway, but you increase your odds and velocity drastically for the other ¾ of the bell curve. You may get turned away by a top candidate who doesn't share your values, but you will gain deep commitment and engagement from those who do. You have to ask yourself: "*If we hire someone who doesn't share our values, is that person going to be a long-term fit anyway?*"

Money talks, of course; but everyone has a price to be stolen away by their competitor, and everyone has a breaking point where no amount of money will retain their loyalty. Most importantly, motivating with money **alone** is almost certain doom to long-term success. Your customers will begin to treat your product/service as a commodity, and your employees are apt to make decisions that advance their **individual short-term interests** rather than **the company's long-term success**.

The best brands in the world understand this. They understand that their product may not be for everyone. However, for their target audience, they have undying customer loyalty and evangelicalism. The best brands understand that not **all** of the top talent is right for their organization. For those who are – those who believe what the company believes – they will not only outperform, but continue to remain loyal and make decisions to benefit the whole rather than for personal gain.

So, how's your brand health? Are you being authentic? Now is a good time to step back, detach yourself from the business, and examine it as an outside consultant. Are your words matching your actions in a way that is *wholly and completely undeniable?* Or are you sending signals (even unintentionally) that are confusing?

Your brand, and your culture, are your reputation. It can change throughout time, but you only get one. With that in mind, I'll leave you with this:

> *"Reputation is like a fragile glass. Once cracked, it's hard to restore its original clarity. It's built with every action and decision, and it's a priceless asset that can open doors or close them." – Unknown*

Notes

1. Shrm. "SHRM Reports Toxic Workplace Cultures Cost Billions." SHRM, 25 Sept. 2019, www.shrm.org/about-shrm/press-room/press-releases/pages/shrm-reports-toxic-workplace-cultures-cost-billions.aspx.

2. Spa Executive. "People Would Take a Pay Cut to Work for an Environmentally Responsible Company." Spa Executive, 23 Mar. 2022, spaexecutive.com/2022/03/23/people-would-take-a-pay-cut-to-work-for-an-environmentally-responsible-company/.

3. https://www.patagonia.com.hk/pages/our-mission

4. Person. "Patagonia Founder Gives Away Company to Help Fight Climate Crisis." Reuters, 16 Sept. 2022, www.reuters.com/business/retail-consumer/patagonia-founder-gives-away-company-help-fight-climate-crisis-2022-09-14/.

5. Jurberg, Ash. "Patagonia Has Provided a Business Blueprint in How to Avoid the Great Resignation." Medium, 26 Nov. 2021, entrepreneurshandbook.co/patagonia-has-provided-a-business-blueprint-in-how-to-avoid-the-great-resignation-6dcd6ea6f668.

6. "State of the Global Workplace Report." Gallup.Com, 20 Feb. 2023, www.gallup.com/workplace/349484/state-of-the-global-workplace-2022-report.aspx.

7. https://www.ted.com/talks/simon_sinek_how_great_leaders_inspire_action?utm_campaign=tedspread&utm_medium=referral&utm_source=tedcomshare

Doug Whitney

Doug Whitney is the Vice President of Marketing at Finit – a CPM/EPM solutions organization that takes pride in prioritizing people over profit. With a focus on brand strategy and digital marketing, Doug is passionate about helping brands tell their story and find their tribes.

Doug is passionate about building teams where everyone thrives and enjoys their working environment, and helping individuals wake up feeling inspired to become the best version of themselves. As a culture leader, Doug has a proven track record of boosting team performance and transforming department culture to make them desirable locations for top talent.

With over a decade of experience in digital marketing and leadership roles, Doug has had many accomplishments, including his role as COO of Model B, a company he helped transform by implementing culture-related initiatives and career path opportunities while doubling revenue per client. Prior to his time at Model B, he received high marks for taking over a struggling media planning team at Quotient, boosting key metrics within six months, and growing the team from six members to sixteen members. He also started a new office for PEP in Minneapolis, MN, servicing General Mills.

Doug is a graduate of UC and, in his free time, enjoys music, basketball, and spending time exploring with his family, including his wife Stefanie and their two amazing sons, Isaac and Lucas.

Connect with Doug Whitney:

LinkedIn: https://www.linkedin.com/in/doug-whitney/

Email: dwhitney87@gmail.com

2.

Intentional Culture Creation

Moving from Vision to Implementation

Karen Hewitt, M. Ed. (Ze/She/They) | Culture Creator, Leader, Writer, Poet, and Artist

We are the culture.

We are culture creators.

We are able to impact and influence workplace culture in meaningful and intentional ways.

I have shifted how I talk about organizations and culture in the last three years. A lot of my experiential knowledge was based on knowing that something was not being done correctly. I learned quite a bit of "what not to do" from my experience in management and supervision in executive leadership. Recently, I have worked to empower leaders and acknowledge the actual impact we can have when we are value-driven, collaborative, and intentional.

This chapter will walk you through a model that takes visionary ideals from what we want culture to be into actionable implementation in our workplace.

For the sake of this chapter, we are defining workplace culture as language, traditions, values, and policies in the organization.

I want to acknowledge from the start that, historically, workplaces have been intentionally designed for the dominant demographic. Historically this has expressed exclusivity through patriarchal, ableist, sexist, racist, neurotypical, and homophobic workplace norms that center the dominant demographic and their comfort. As the workplace diversifies, so too should our design of workplace culture.

The key question sits at the heart of this chapter: If we impact and influence workplace culture in meaningful and intentional ways; what can that do for those working there, for the output of the office, and/or for the ability of that workplace to influence other workplaces?

Reimagining the workplace

The process starts with a vision: not just a noun, but a verb that we must use to begin to formulate the cultural layout that will enable everyone to thrive in the workplace.

As I envision what type of workplace culture I want to create, I am invited into the visionary space. This space requires me to be connected with: my longing for community and passion-driven work, my creativity, my compassion, my lived experiences, and my knowing of what is possible. The visionary space has no limits on what can be created. In this space, I am resourced, imaginative, innovative, and ready to dream.

Once I have visualized what is ideal, I can then sift through what remains to see what is tangible and I can logistically work to make things so in the strategic and implementation space. As we move towards implementation, we must continue to revisit the vision to ensure that implementation is achievable, and that we are working towards that. We stay aligned and in service as we move towards implementation of that vision into our workplace culture.

Let's take a look at what it means to have vision. I will share questions to ask yourself and your leadership team for your reflection. From there, we will take a look at what language, traditions, values, and policies exist. We should also examine what needs to be implemented in service of this vision. We will then examine what sustainability looks like.

The areas of exploration in culture creation are:

1. Creating the Learning Environment
2. Diversity, Equity, Inclusion, and Accessibility
3. Employee Wellness
4. Accountability

If you begin to intentionally curate the culture you want to see in these four areas, you will start to see transformative shifts in yourself and your organization as a whole.

Creating The Learning Environment

My biggest shift in the workplace environment as a manager was in operations at a factory supervising temporary employees. The policies were strict and evidenced zero tolerance for divergence. Still, employees continuously violated the rules.

At times, I felt like I had no control over *not* terminating employees if they violated a policy. Over time, I started to get more curious. Employees started talking to me and I began to understand the reasons why people were struggling in the workplace. Right beneath the tardies, call-offs, and missed targets on their productivity, there were opportunities: opportunities for both coaching and learning moments.

When I leaned into the conversations I was having with the employees and started seeking solutions *with* them for the root problems, I started to see a shift in their commitment to the workplace. Many of them eventually transitioned to full-time employment. They didn't need someone to cut them off the moment they did something out of compliance. They needed someone to listen and give them some room to learn and grow from missteps.

Shifting from a zero-tolerance environment to a learning environment is challenging. It requires more from us as leaders. It asks us to be more compassionate, more patient, and to do our due diligence when it comes to coaching. We have to see what is available to us and be committed to our own growth, development, and creative abilities.

Zero-tolerance environments create fear and rigidity. The learning environment is a commitment to the individual and the collective that promises that repair is available. There is psychological safety in knowing that you don't have to show up perfectly. There is also an advocacy component that invites us to speak up for those who have less influence and power and make sure the workplace culture centers the dignity of all of those who work in the organization.

The learning environment requires infrastructure that supports the room needed for the Right Relationship. "Right Relationship" comes from the Principle of Oneness, stating that we are all connected, and we impact each other. Right Relationship is about being aligned and in integrity with yourself and others.[1]

I often think of "Right Relationship," in its ideal state, as the recycle sign in action interpersonally. To govern this space of alignment, we create agreements instead of rules. We are intentional about language in our internal and external communications. We call each other in when there is a misstep. Calling in is often used when people want to compassionately inform someone that what they've said or done is problematic, harmful and not okay.[2] We interrogate our policies and collaborate on collective values.

In our own visioning about the learning environment, we must ask ourselves specific questions about what our ideal environment looks like. As you visualize, this is a space where honesty – sometimes brutal – is invited. There is nuance in creating space and also creating healthy workplace boundaries in your infrastructure. We will focus on the nuance and boundaries in the implementation space.

Visionary Reflection Questions:

1. Why is creating the learning environment important for me and those who work in this space?
2. How do I define development and growth?
3. What is my role in coaching and developing my team?

4. What opportunities are there for employees to develop and advance in this organization?
5. What has my experience been with zero-tolerance policies, and how has that impacted how I supervise?
6. In what ways have I been shown compassion and understanding in a learning environment?
7. How do I want to show up with compassion and flexibility?
8. How do I manage performance metrics in this conversation?
9. What are my non-negotiable agreements in this space?
10. What shared language would be helpful in this space for me and my team?
11. What does collaborative communication look like in this environment?
12. What training do I need to be a more effective coach?

Implementation

After reflection, it is time to see what can be implemented. Visioning is a vital step in the process, but if you stop there, nothing has changed. First, you need to think about power.

Power dynamics have a role in this conversation. It is important to know how much power you have to influence change. You may not have the power to be able to shift company-wide culture immediately. Instead, you can influence change in your department/team directly; then, as people and productivity shifts positively, you find ways to share these stories on a more macro level.

Language: I generally start with language. It is the most subtle but influential change you can make. Even if you don't announce that you are starting to use more empowering language, people will experience your shift in language in a positive way.

See what language you can use to create an affirming space. For example:

- Celebrate those that are fully present or complete projects.
- Thank them for sharing when they contribute.
- Celebrate when one of their ideas is utilized and implemented.
- Ask them how you can support them when they seem to be struggling with a deadline or project management.
- Schedule regular check-ins with your team where you earnestly ask how they are doing and provide direction and support. Honor these one-on-ones on your calendar and try to avoid canceling them.

Next, think about how you run your meetings and whose voices get heard more than not. What methods and platforms of communication exist for introverts and internal processors? Across a range of studies, nonverbal communication is 70-90 percent of our communication.[3]

So, what does your body language say? Ultimately, language can have an incredibly significant impact on how people experience the environment. If you want it to truly be a learning environment, the language you use – both verbal and nonverbal – will have to embody that.

Values: Give some intentional thought to values. The main reason it is important to know your own values and your organization's values so deeply is to make sure that they are in alignment. If values conflict, then when there is challenge, it is hard to reconcile if one party is asking the other to disregard their value and belief system.

What are your personal values? What are your organizational values? Does your team see these values posted anywhere visually?

As you acknowledge the various individual value systems at play, this will be important to consider when you are making agreements, our teams' individual and collective non-negotiables in the workplace. Let the awareness of your and the teams' values govern what you all value as a collective.

Traditions: Another space to create a culture shift is with traditions. We don't have to do what this particular department in question has always done. If pizza parties don't motivate this team, but half-days off on a Friday do, let's rethink how we celebrate wins. If previous culture asked everyone to come into work even when they may be showing symptoms of illness, we can find ways to model and encourage people to utilize their sick days and not put people at risk by coming in. We can encourage those who may be sick not to work hybrid when they should actually rest and heal. If we have a team of folks that struggle with executive function and deadlines, maybe we incorporate a visible calendar where people can see everyone's deadline, or a to-do list we all can access.

Traditions are the perpetual and consistent ways we approach things when there is a specific stimulus. What traditions and practices exist currently, and how can you shift them to encourage growth and development?

Policy: Policies are the easiest to change when you have power to influence change. A lot of policy changes can get caught up in red tape heading to executive leadership. This is why culture always prevails interdepartmentally. However, if we want sustainable change, then we have to keep working to get policies codified that benefit the learning environment. Some policies that directly impact the learning environment are:

- attendance policies
- budget and access to professional development opportunities
- performance metric policies
- bonus structures
- PTO policies
- grievance policies
- tuition reimbursement

Do the policies you currently have invite folks to be flexible, understanding, consistent, rigorous, and their best selves? Or do the policies invite rigid and punitive ways of being?

Your policies are often the first thing people see when they are onboarding. What do your policies say about the workplace?

The learning environment is the framework for how your team operates, how they communicate with each other, and how they view growth and development opportunities. Being intentional in this space takes time and attention. It also requires collaboration. This will be a mindset shift for many, so give yourself some grace as you pioneer this new approach. If you already work in a place that has a healthy learning environment, show your gratitude and keep visioning and implementing ways to make it more affirming.

Diversity, Equity, Inclusion, and Accessibility

We can all acknowledge that diversity, equity, inclusion, and accessibility have been under the magnifying-glass lens since the murder of George Floyd, the pandemic, and national racial and social unrest. Though DEI has been in existence for over twenty years, the field has shifted significantly in the last three years.

People are longing for connection more than they ever have. Many want to know that, at minimum, their workplace is safe. People want to experience connection, safety, belonging, and a strong central focus on their own human dignity. For a true culture shift, DEIA should be woven into the very fabric of the workplace. Language, values, traditions, and policies should affirm that people are requested to be present as their full and authentic selves with all of their intersections and identities.

In our own visioning of diversity, equity, inclusion, and accessibility, we have to get incredibly honest with ourselves. We must put in the work to examine all of our biases as they will inevitably show up as we reflect.

The good news about the visionary reflection process is that you don't have to announce your bias to everyone; you just have to be willing to acknowledge that it unquestionably exists. This is a process we call interrogation. Interrogation can have a negative connotation, but, ideally, it is an invitation. Interrogation asks that we set down our ego and judgment and get very curious about the ways we have always done things historically in our organization and team.

Visionary Reflection Questions for DEIA

1. Historically, who has held power in this organization?
2. Who influences power now?
3. How do I leverage my access to power and influence change?
4. How do I define diversity, equity, inclusion, and

accessibility?

5. Why is this work important to me?

6. How do I appreciate folks with a different lived experience than me?

7. What relationships exist in my life with people that don't look like me?

8. Am I aware of my biases and working to acknowledge them and address them?

9. As is, who would feel safe and included in this workplace culture?

10. What voices are missing in this department and organization?

11. Whose voice and lived experience do I want to center in this department and organization?

12. Do I have any fear about including more diversity in this department or organization?

13. What does our forward-facing messaging about the organization say about our commitment to DEIA?

14. Do we take action and invest in creating a more diverse organization?

15. What are the benefits of diversity, inclusion, and accessibility?

Implementation

Language: Again, we start with language. If your organization has no statement or images on your website attracting and affirming diversity, then that itself is a message. Though you may be trying to be aspirational, if your forward-facing messaging (social media, website, marketing materials) misrepresents the actual diversity present in your organization, then, it is representing a culture that does not exist. This misrepresentation could potentially attract folks that presume a certain level of safety and inclusion who then experience something completely different.

We are responsible for the language we use and the messaging we have. Employees can *feel* the difference between tolerance and affirmation. Those who have identities in several, historically underrepresented diversity dimensions [4], will also know when they are the token representative. Get very clear on who you want to work there, and who you want to lead, and then provide access to lead there. The way you talk about diversity internally and externally will create the workplace culture organically.

Values: As you navigate the language that your organization and team use around diversity, value alignment in the DEIA space is essential. The biggest challenge in the workplace can be when senior leadership does not have the same values as the rest of the organization. We all have values and beliefs about DEIA, but if we don't value them as integral to the success of our workplace community, then we will struggle as an organization. If there is a disconnect in commitment to DEIA between senior leadership and those they are leading, it will be felt at all levels. Those who are not in the dominant demographic will likely feel it most, and recruitment and retention will doubtlessly suffer.

Traditions: The beauty of culture as we know it from ethnicity and indigenous lens is that there are so many different takes on traditions. It is important to see which traditions can be collaborative, culturally sensitive, and responsive.[5] This can look like the holidays we celebrate and/or are given off. How do we celebrate or acknowledge when a teammate is celebrating an important and non-American holiday or cultural celebration?

It is also important to think of how we create space for grief and processing. There are a lot of local, national, and global current events that are incredibly traumatic and specific to a certain subset of our employees. How do we care for people when they are experiencing fear, sadness, or grief?

What about food? If we have team lunches, do we make sure that we honor the diets of everyone attending?

Traditions can get more granular the more globally we think about it. Try to stay connected to the identities present in your team and get comfortable and familiarize yourself with their cultural traditions. Collaborate on ones that will support inclusion and belonging on your team and within your organization.

Policy: This area is so significant for DEIA. Is DEIA seen as a learning development checklist, or is it seen as cultural values that are lived out in action? Are there performance metrics assigned to DEIA specifically?

How policy is set up around this will determine how seriously people take efforts of diversity, equity, inclusion, and accessibility. ADA (The Americans with Disabilities Act) compliance is something that must be considered. This determines, very literally, who can be in the space.

Truly interrogate your policies around the following:

- objectives and goals to increase diversity
- grievance policies
- parental leave
- nursing/pumping accommodations
- Parking accommodations for new parents
- gender neutral bathrooms
- sick leave
- PTO
- flexible work environment and hybrid opportunities
- opportunities for advancement vs. personal improvement plans
- equity policies
- philanthropic ventures and partners
- community service

With any policy, getting into data analysis here is supportive. Understanding where retention is suffering and addressing those deficits is key.

Policies can create buy-in. This is especially true when they are interconnected with compensation. Policies can set the tone for the inclusive space that you actually want in your organization and let people know from the beginning that they are intentionally considered and cared for in this organization.

Key Questions: Do you have policies around pronouns being in your email signature? Does your organization have clear parental leave policies? Does your space have gender-neutral bathrooms? Do you at least have conversations or training about it in learning and development? What diversity dimensions are seen as an annoyance? How do you keep up with current and relevant issues in DEIA?[6]

Employee Wellness

This category is specific to the prioritization of employee wellness in your organization. Historically, people have called this work-life balance. These aren't just buzzwords or phrases. They're far more than that. The hope is that visualizing and then implementing prioritized practices centering around wellness will lead to work-life *harmony*.

We can get caught up in performance metrics, productivity, and our bottom line and forsake the well-being of our employees. As we move out of the pandemic – arguably the most traumatic collective event of our time – it is important to start to interrogate our ways of being and our organizational relationship to social, emotional, and mental wellness.

Visionary Reflection Questions:

1. How do we talk about social, emotional, and mental wellness?
2. What would it look like to model behaviors that prioritize personal wellness?
3. In what ways do perfectionism, productivity, and endurance show up as primary values for this organization?
4. What tools and resources are available for folks in the organization that are having a hard time socially, emotionally, and/or mentally?
5. What are healthy communication styles and practices around discussing our personal wellness in this organization?
6. What amount of our budget is allotted for development that centers restoration for our employees?
7. Are the demands of this workplace reasonable?
8. What policies exist that make it challenging for people to get what they need in terms of their own wellness?
9. What things have I struggled with, and what support systems did I wish existed for my own well-being?
10. Who experiences the most barriers around accessing wellness care in our organization?

Implementation

Language: There is a lot of stigma in the language surrounding wellness. The terms "crazy" or "insane" often get thrown around for people who are expressing an emotional need. We have to consider the impact of how we speak about people who utilize their voices to state what is going on with them outside of work. Our social and emotional state of being significantly impacts our ability to show up as our best selves in the workplace. The language used, especially by senior leadership and in organizational messaging, will always set the tone for the workplace culture of health and wellness.

Values: Wellness could actually be a value in your organization, but if it is not modeled, then people will create their own culture around it. If the leader is always coming to work when they're sick, or sending emails at all hours of the night and day, then people will start to think that is what is needed to succeed in the organization. It is important to model employee wellness for our team to believe that it is also okay to care for themselves.

Traditions: Other important values in this conversation include: communication, collaboration, and teamwork. If people do not have the certainty that they can care for themselves and that their leader and team will have their back, then they will consistently feel guilty for taking care of their wellness needs. The traditions of how we deal with social, emotional, and mental health needs in our team and organization will develop as people start to make conclusions about what is important based on what the organization actually communicates.

Policy: Wellness policies are crucial to the employee's ability to stay well. The policies that should be interrogated are:

- PTO
- EAP (Employee Assistance Programs) access
- wellness spending options
- wellness initiatives in the organization
- policies for work missed while out and negotiable deadlines
- advancement opportunities
- grievance mediation

The key question is this: how are we empowering ourselves as leaders, and those who report to us, in caring for themselves so they can show up as their best selves?

Accountability

Oftentimes accountability in an organization does not get addressed, especially at the senior leadership level. There is a paralyzing fear about the effects that accountability might have on the individual. So, it becomes much easier to pass on the blame to someone in a reporting position than to take accountability for missteps.

Accountability is hard. A culture of accountability asks that the ego not be present and that we commit to what is right and best for the organization over personal guilt or shame. This can be especially difficult when bottom-line dollars are at stake. These positions are our livelihood, and accountability has historically meant getting fired, followed by the possibility of poor recommendations to pursue other employment.

Visionary Reflection Questions:

1. What is our organization's relationship with accountability?
2. How have you experienced accountability with your supervisors?
3. Are compassion and grace available?
4. What are the practices around tracking and documentation?
5. Do you feel comfortable owning your personal missteps?
6. Do you know of any organizations that are doing accountability well?
7. How important is trust as a value for you and your organization?
8. What if you could trust yourself and your team to be radically responsible and accountable for their work and how they show up?

Implementation

Language: If we are committed to the learning environment, then workplace culture around accountability must be consistent throughout the entirety of the organization. If we do not talk about accountability internally, then people will not find it important. If we do not talk about it externally, then the community and clients we serve will not trust our brand.

The last three years have given many organizations ample opportunities to be accountable for missteps. An organization's ability to recover is key to how they are viewed moving forward. Think of an organization that has had a misstep recently.

Now think about the forward-facing messaging that was created to address said misstep. What was your perception of that organization after the misstep? What was your perception of the organization following the creation of its forward-facing messaging? How we acknowledge and accept accountability speaks directly to our integrity as an individual and an organization.

Values: As a value, motivation can be simple around why people take accountability seriously. Sometimes it is just about not losing business. Other times there is a deep commitment to being in Right Relationship (being aligned and in integrity with yourself and others). It is important to know your personal and organizational commitments when it comes to accountability. This commitment will govern how you respond and what action you take when a misstep occurs.

Traditions: The traditions you create and allow around accountability will ultimately be a part of your legacy. What will people say about your values and traditions towards accountability when you leave the organization? What does truly embodying integrity look like in your role and in your sphere of influence?

Policy: Execution of policies with regard to accountability is vital. How employees, supervisors, senior leadership, and board of trustee members are held accountable matters. If there are policies that create a double standard in action, they must be interrogated and swiftly changed.

Policies that directly deal with accountability are:

- performance reviews
- supervisor/employee relationships
- team dynamics around communication of a misstep
- grievance policies
- mediation and internal investigations
- communications and marketing materials
- documentation
- PTO policies

Key Questions: Are there processes in place that support the learning environment when it comes to accountability? Are there different standards of accountability depending on your position in the organization? Is repair available, and when is it not available?

Moving Forward

This chapter walked us through a visionary reflection process for the workplace culture categories of:

1. Creating the Learning Environment
2. Diversity, Equity, Inclusion, and Accessibility
3. Employee Wellness
4. Accountability

There may be areas specific to your organization that don't seem to fall under one of the categories covered here. This process of visionary reflection will allow you to sit with what would be ideal for your organization and then work to intentionally implement as much of that as possible into your team and organizational culture.

We are culture creators in the workplace. That is not in question. The question is: what type of workplace culture are you creating?

Notes

1. Brandwashed. "In Right Relationship." Coralus, Formerly SheEO, 4 Sept. 2020, coralus.world/in-right-relationship/#:~:text=The%20idea%20of%20%27being%20in,no%20such%20thing%20as%20externalities.

2. Dainkeh, Fatima. "Calling in vs. Calling out: When and How to Use One Approach over the Other in the Workplace." She+ Geeks Out, 13 Feb. 2023, www.shegeeksout.com/blog/calling-in-vs-calling-out-when-and-how-to-use-one-approach-over-the-other-in-the-workplace/.

3. Spence, Jacq. "Nonverbal Communication: How Body Language & Nonverbal Cues Are Key." Lifesize, 5 Mar. 2021, www.lifesize.com/blog/speaking-without-words/#:~:text=What%20percentage%20of%20communication%20is,of%20all%20communication%20is%20nonverbal.

4. https://www.usydanthology.com/2019/04/12/lodens-wheel-of-diversity/

5. Ahmed, Anam. "What Practices Could You Implement to Increase Cultural Sensitivity & Acceptance in the Workplace?" Small Business - Chron.Com, 18 Oct. 2019, smallbusiness.chron.com/practices-could-implement-increase-cultural-sensitivity-acceptance-workplace-16661.html.

6. https://www.usydanthology.com/2019/04/12/lodens-wheel-of-diversity/

Karen Hewitt

Karen earned her MS in Mathematics at St. Francis University (PA) and her Master of Arts in Educational Policy and Leadership at The Ohio State University. Ze has been speaking, facilitating, and coaching since 2005. Her career began as a collegiate Women's Basketball Coach and evolved into a Workforce Development focus. Her areas of expertise are: Culture and Diversity Management, Leadership Development, Intersectionality, and Gender and Sexuality.

Karen is a creative. She is an improv comedian and improv poet, and singer. She is a 2020 recipient of the Create Columbus Visionary Award, a 2022 CEO Columbus Future 50 fellow, a 2023 African – American Leadership Academy (AALA) fellow, a 2021 Cohort Poet in Scott Woods' Rhapsody and Refrain, and an ensemble member in Counterfeit Madison's Aretha Franklin Tribute; which performed in front of a sold-out Lincoln Theatre (Columbus, Ohio) in February

2020. In 2019, Karen published hir first book of poetry, Grounded: A Collection of Healing Spoken Word Poetry, and released: Fire: Poetic Memoirs of a Movement in August of 2021. They are also a contributing author with their top five lessons in love and business chapters in the April 2021 released anthology, The Black Woman's Guide To Love and Business: A Blueprint To Self-Mastery.

Karen lives in Columbus, Ohio, with her wife, Erin, and cat, Temple.

Connect with Karen Hewitt:

LinkedIn: https://www.linkedin.com/in/karen-hewitt-m-ed-13b07128/

Email: khewittconsulting@gmail.com

3.

Becoming an Award-Winning Workplace

Angie Redmon | Workplace Advisor, HR Coach and Culture Coach

Imagine having candidates reach out to you to apply for your job posting rather than you having to spend countless hours searching for them.

Imagine a pool of talent wanting to work at your organization because their friends and others in their network told them about your organization.

Imagine that the retention rate of your employees is consistently high because they not only think they work for a great organization, but couldn't imagine working anywhere else.

I've been there. I've seen what happens when organizations are intentional about their recruitment and retention strategies. As a result, their leadership and HR teams become significantly more impactful because they are forward thinking, resolution-driven, and focused on the future.

I have over twenty-five years of HR experience, and I've seen and learned invaluable lessons during that period of time. I've learned how to lead a phenomenal workplace culture and I've also seen when things were not done as well. During my years of experience, I've learned more from the times when things were not done as well, and didn't go as planned. This makes doing things right all that more important.

My career began in staffing where I worked with many organizations and employees in various industries and sizes. I hired hundreds of employees and unfortunately had my fair share of terminations as well. The most impactful learning experience I had during my decade spent in staffing was my exposure to "*Kaizen*:" a Japanese term meaning change for the better or continuous improvement.

My introduction to Kaizen prepared me to be intentional about continuous improvement. I witnessed firsthand how focusing on the improvement of even just one area can make a significant impact on the organization as a whole.

The years spent in staffing helped me to learn many aspects of Operations and HR, yet I yearned to be part of an organization. With staffing, I would send employees to their job sites and wait to hear back from them about how they felt the job was going. Or, I would hear from the supervisor on how the employee was performing. I did have a few years where I worked on-site in the locations where I placed employees, with my desk alongside the managers for that company. I wanted to take it a step further and see how things worked from the "inside." I wanted to work for the same common goals as those employees that I hired and placed. My next step was to set out to find my corporate home.

Fortunately, it didn't take long for me to get hired at a fast-paced technology organization as an HR Director. I knew during that first interview that this was the company I wanted to work for. The people were amazing, friendly, and appeared to be incredibly talented. The environment was fast-paced, energetic, and seemed fun. The work was a perfect match for me to apply what I had learned after a decade in staffing to support this organization as their HR Director.

My career evolved into leadership roles in HR from growing a team of one to a team of multiple employees (I did this more than once), mergers and acquisitions (M&A) activity, working in both private and public organizations. My responsibilities and expertise were vast, yet one thing remained constant: my focus on workplace culture. This was always a pillar for my work. With each new opportunity, I focused on how we could consistently make the workplace culture better, and how we could continuously improve what was already great.

With my focus on workplace culture, appreciation for continuous improvement, and a calling to help others, I knew there had to be something more for me. Although I loved the work I was doing, I wanted to hone in on how to consistently improve workplace cultures. At this point, I had spent years studying employee engagement, analyzing engagement surveys that employees completed and interpreting how those surveys' responses could be applied to improve the workplace. I already had success with this in my corporate seat, and now it was time to help other organizations do the same. And there I had it; my company, striveHR, was born.

I have learned a tremendous amount of what was needed to improve workplace culture through studying employee engagement. It's amazing what your employees will share with you if you simply take the time to ask and listen. Most importantly, organizations that intentionally focus on their cultures, dedicate time and energy towards employee engagement, and make people-strategy a top priority have one thing in common: they often become award-winning workplaces.

Let's look at what workplace awards are, why you may consider becoming an award-winning workplace, and how to make that happen.

Workplace Awards

Workplace awards recognize organizations who are outstanding in their industry or in their geographic area for their workplace culture. These awards are measured by evaluating the organization, often through an employee engagement survey, and comparing those results against others in their same category.

Organizations are interested in earning workplace awards for a number of reasons. Primarily, they apply for these awards to elevate their brand, leverage the recognition they receive from this award to attract talent to their company, and to have a deeper understanding of why their employees like working for their organization and stay there.

Many organizations who earn these awards will tell you that it is their #1 resource for recruiting candidates. Before launching my business, I led the HR team for a fast-growing organization where recruitment was a constant focal point. As our company grew, we needed to find top-notch candidates that would be great additions to our team. One morning I met with a group of new employees during their first day of orientation. When I asked how they heard about our company, two-thirds of these new employees stated they went to the Best Place to Work list and saw our company name. This validated our efforts towards achieving a Best Place to Work status in an effort to support our recruitment.

I often hear from organizations who have won a workplace award that they see consistent benefits from earning this distinction. So, I was curious about what kept other organizations from applying. I conducted a survey with a group of HR professionals to measure their knowledge of workplace awards. I asked them to check off which of these statements best applied to them, and here are those respondents' replies:

We applied, won the award and are enjoying the benefits of being recognized.	5%
We applied, but did not win. We plan to try again.	5%
I've heard of workplace awards but I do not have executive buy-in to apply.	14%
I've heard of workplace awards but I have no idea where to start.	76%

When I conducted this survey, I anticipated the concern over executive buy-in would be higher based on previous conversations I've had with HR professionals. What surprised me was the high response to:

I've heard of workplace awards, but I have no idea where to start.

Yes, you saw that correctly – 76% of HR professionals in this survey do not know where to start. This number illustrates that they know awards are out there, and chances are good that they know there are benefits to getting a workplace award. However, navigating the *how* within this process stops them before they ever really get started.

Define your WHY

Knowing where to get started to become an award-winning workplace begins well before the actual nomination or application. It's not simply that you, as a company or organization, apply for an award and "wait and see" what happens. You need to have a strong reason to apply to be recognized as an award-winning workplace. Your intentionality will serve as a key driver for you.

I've met with organizations who list earning a workplace award as part of their corporate goals and strategic plan. This takes time, resources and – for some – a financial commitment. There are going to be times on this journey when you have to make a tough decision as to where your priorities are.

When deciding to apply to become an award-winning workplace, the first focus is your WHY. The reason you are considering applying is your WHY. It identifies what you want to improve, to be known or recognized for.

Your WHY could be:

- Improving your ability to attract and keep top talent.
- Addressing a concern your organization is experiencing, such as a toxic culture or misaligned direction.
- Increasing market awareness and credibility.

A great place to start in uncovering your WHY is to identify what pain points your organization is currently facing. Think of challenges your organization is facing that need to be addressed. Are there goals that have been set that you are struggling to meet? What are some issues that are taking place that negatively impact your workforce?

Let's face it – most business leaders and HR professionals have plenty to do. Days are filled with more work than there are hours to get it all done. Adding one more thing to your plate, such as applying for a workplace award, may overload an already full to-do list. You may see there are opportunities for improvement within your organization but are too busy with your day-to-day to consider this a priority.

Or, you may already work for an organization with a great corporate culture. Although you may not have glaring pain points to address, you want to recognize your employees and organization for creating a great environment.

Understanding there are benefits to earning a workplace award distinction helps with narrowing in on your WHY and gives you direction when your daily responsibilities and other priorities cause distractions.

Benefits of Becoming an Award-Winning Workplace

Now that you have learned what workplace awards are, and you understand the importance of defining your WHY, you may be asking yourself: Is it worth all the work?

Although each organization may have a specific reason to apply, they need to see a benefit in order to continue on with the process. There are many benefits and perks to getting recognized as an award-winning workplace.

Applying for a workplace award will likely include conducting an employee engagement survey conducted by the award program administrator. The findings of this survey will be your roadmap to areas you are seeking to improve as a company. When these improvements are made, you will be on the path to enjoying the benefits of becoming an award-winning workplace.

To answer the question, Is it worth all the work? Yes, I believe it is, and here are the benefits you may receive from doing that work.

1. **Strengthens Employee Engagement**. Your employees want to be heard. By asking for their feedback, you are opening the door for connection. You are giving them an opportunity to share their voice, their ideas, as well as their concerns. By asking for and receiving that feedback, you are enhancing their feeling of value, trust,

and impact.

2. **Aligning Initiatives to Strategic Goals.** Understanding the connection between strategic goals, department goals, and what employees do each day to achieve corporate goals helps align the organization. Your employees will see the direct connection between what they do every day and how it contributes to the organization as a whole. It brings "How am I making a difference?" and "What do I do that impacts the greater good?" to the forefront.

3. **Communication Roadmap.** When you conduct an employee engagement survey, you will receive a tremendous amount of data to analyze, act upon, and share with your employees. This process will give you the tools to learn how your employees feel about working for your company and will showcase key initiatives that you can begin working on to increase employee engagement. This ultimately creates long-lasting, positive change within your company.

4. **Empower Employees**. Allow your employees to become decision-makers. Often, employees on the frontline have the best ideas. If you want to know how to achieve a better, more efficient, and productive way to do the job, simply ask those who are already doing the work.

5. **Customer Impact**. If your employees are engaged in their work, and feel empowered to make decisions, they will take care of your customers to the best of their abilities. Take care of your employees and you will see it reflected on your bottom line.

6. **Bragging Rights**. This goes beyond having a shiny trophy to display in your lobby, or a flashy logo to put on the "careers" page of your website. Imagine how proud your employees will feel when they tell others in their network that they work for an organization who earns awards for their workplace culture.

For a full description for each benefit, visit https://strivehr.net/award.

Process of Applying for An Award

As strong of a connection as I have with continuous improvement, I equally like a good process.

I've talked with many organizations who have different approaches to how they apply for their workplace awards. What I have found to be successful for those who have not only earned, but maintained, their workplace award is to stick with a strong process for doing so.

There are three important steps to take before you even submit an application for an award.

1. **Define and understand your WHY**. We have already reviewed in depth the reasons for defining your why. This is perhaps the most important step to take, even before you apply. This will be the rock that you will

center your process around.

2. **Willingness to be patient**. I often use the word "journey" when describing this process of becoming an award-winning workplace. Simply put: it's not a quick, overnight accomplishment. If done properly, you are going through all the necessary steps to establish your foundation and your accountability to this work, and to your employees.

3. **Commit to the work ahead**. Let's face it, if getting a workplace award was easy, every organization would be included in a workplace awards list. Your leadership team is going to need to dedicate time and resources to this initiative. Also, commit to sharing the results with your employees, and support the efforts needed to embrace continuous improvement for your company.

Awareness

Now that you have moved through the three pre-survey steps, it's time to decide what award you would like to apply for. There are several items to consider when making this decision. Think of what you are wanting to achieve by winning this award. Are you looking to be recognized within your geographic area or industry? Are you looking for local or national recognition?

Often, engagement survey administrators will provide sample questions so that your company/organization can see what type of information they are evaluating. Some administrators will also provide you with the ability to customize questions; keep in mind that this is often for an upcharge. Most surveys will include open-ended questions. These open-ended questions will give you additional insight about your employees and will also dig deeper into topics that may not have been addressed in survey questions.

Why select one award over the other? I encourage you to tie this back to your WHY. Is the one you selected going to help you to achieve the benefits you are seeking? Do you meet the requirements to apply for that award? Many will have a minimum employee count required to apply. Be sure to check into these before making your selection.

The survey administrator will likely offer an outline of expected "next steps;" which could include an employer application and employee engagement survey. Along this process you will note additional requirements that need to be met in order to proceed. These can include a minimum participation rate on the employee engagement survey.

Administration

The employee engagement survey is the heart of this award process. Employee engagement surveys are your pulse into finding out what your employees think about working for your company. It's an opportunity for them to have an anonymous avenue to share their concerns and ideas.

Conducting an employee engagement survey creates a safe place where your employees can voice their opinions. Many of the survey administrators have gone to great lengths to ensure anonymity and confidentiality for your employees to share their feedback. Employees can be sensitive to sharing feedback that is not positive (think constructive feedback). Your employees don't want to be shunned or looked upon negatively because they opened up about their concerns.

The engagement surveys are a powerful way to gauge how your employees feel about working for your organization. You will gather insights into key factors to help you make decisions impacting your business and people operations. You will get a baseline for your organization's corporate culture. After all, it's difficult to determine what to work on and measure improvement if you don't know where you stand.

Acknowledgment

After the employee engagement survey is conducted, and the survey administrator reviews all the submissions and evaluates the scores, it's time to notify organizations if they have achieved the designation of an award-winning workplace. During this time, it is natural to think only about the award, but I caution you to keep going back to your WHY. Why did you administer an employee engagement survey? What problem are you trying to solve? What improvement(s) are you hoping to make? Your engagement survey data and findings will yield what you need to do.

Winning the award, although it is incredibly nice, isn't the only reason you did this. Whatever the outcome, remember your WHY. If you won – take time to celebrate! There are so many clever ways to share this celebration with your employees. If you did not win – tell your employees. Don't hide it because you will lose trust with them.

Action

Whether you did or did not win, go back to your commitment to the work. It's time to take action to review what you learned through this process. You are in this for the long haul. Learning insights to act upon is more valuable than earning the trophy. You will have come full circle by conducting the survey. You will have identified what you did well and what you need to work on, shared results, addressed areas of improvement, and measured your success. Use the information obtained to better your company/organization.

What To Do With All That Data

After your survey closes, you will receive your engagement survey reports. There will be a lot of information, and it is natural to feel overwhelmed by this. More than one leader has confessed to me that they did not review their engagement reports. They shared that there was too much to review and that they needed to focus their time on the other responsibilities within their job. And yet, what was their reaction after making that statement? Regret. They wished they had taken the time to review what their employees said so that they could react and respond.

There is a tremendous amount of data and information in the engagement survey reports. Although different administrators will package the reports in different ways, you likely will get a high-level executive summary along with detailed reports by department and tenure, for example. Topics such as benefits, compensation, leadership, training, development, and more will be covered. Some will also offer specialized reports such as DE&I. Consider this a gold mine of data. It's absolutely worth the time to review these reports to understand how your employees feel about your organization and what areas they would like to see improved.

One section of data that will be very useful for you are the open-ended comments. Here, your employees can further explain their responses. Some reviewers admit to skimming over the open-ended comments when reviewing the data without digging deep into them. Why? Because it is time consuming. There may be hundreds of open-ended comments, depending on the number of employees responding to the survey. There is a lot of value in these comments as they may provide clarity to other sections of the survey. It is well-worth the time to read them thoroughly.

Now that you have all that data, it's time to do something with it. You may be tempted to work on every area that needs improvement, but that is not realistic. Identify three to five areas for improvement. The areas you choose will depend on the number of items to be addressed, and the number of team members you have to support improvement areas. Taking on too much will leave you frustrated and you will likely be disappointed that you couldn't tackle it all.

Once you have the results of the survey, you may be wondering which areas to focus on. The reports may clearly show opportunities for improvement, however, it's best to work with an experienced professional to help navigate the data. Although you may see areas that rank higher in properties of focus when digging through the data you may find that there could be underlying information that helps to point the focus in another direction.

It's also very important to consider your organization's strategic goals. Does the engagement data support the goals your organization has set? Is there a connection between what you learned from the survey's findings to what goals your company is actively working on? The answer to these questions are helpful to consider when determining the three areas of focus.

After you have analyzed your data and determined what you would like to work towards improving, it's time to create a communication plan!

Communication is Key

Your organization has invested time and resources into your employee engagement survey and towards your initiative to become an award-winning workplace. You want to make sure you are getting valuable feedback from your employees. To be most effective, you will want to create a communication strategy of messaging to share with your employees before, during, and after the engagement survey. Your communication should include what your employees can expect during this process.

Your employees took the time to share their opinions and thoughts with you in your survey. Identifying how you will communicate what you have learned to all employees, including the executive team, managers and staff, is imperative to the success of your experience with this initiative.

Simply put: a strong communication plan is key.

Executive Summary

The executive and leadership teams will be the first to hear the findings from the engagement survey; before you present them to your employees. It is likely that they will not want all the details that are included in full reports.

They are expecting to receive:

- Highlights of the survey, both the positive aspects as well as improvement areas.
- Specific topics of concern that will require more action and attention.
- Your recommendations for improvement, as well as how these connect to the organizations' strategic goals.

Be sure to include highlights of "wins." These wins could include areas of improvement from a previous survey, topics which you have been striving to improve within your organization, or pleasant surprises from the results.

An important talking point to discuss with the leadership team is your organization's rollout plan. This is where you will be addressing strategies to share the data with your employees including who will deliver the information, when and where this information will be shared, and how the data will be presented.

Employee Presentation

The first thing to share with your employees is a sincere "THANK YOU!" Thank them for responding to the survey, regardless of the result. Without your employees' involvement in this initiative, you would be missing out on valuable feedback.

Sharing the outcome of the award application and the findings of your employee engagement survey is often done at the company-wide level. Consider including the following items in the presentation:

- Areas where the organization scored well
- Items to be worked on
- Goals set based on the survey findings
- Employee involvement in focus groups/teams to address improvement ideas (if determined by your organization)
- Addressing employee questions
- Next steps

The biggest mistake that can be made after receiving the survey's findings is to avoid sharing the data with your employees. If organizational leaders elect to not share the results of the survey, or avoid keeping employees updated during the process, they will ensure that employees will not participate in surveys in the future. Lack of communication creates a lack of trust with your employees.

Circle Back On Progress

As demonstrated in the 4 As Wheel (Awareness, Administration, Acknowledgement, Action), the process is a continuous one; and it is continuous by design. The momentum built from asking questions before and during the engagement survey, to acknowledging the results (and if you won the award), to taking action to understand the results, report back and analyze progress naturally means this process continues.

Measuring your progress will be key during your action steps.

First, bring the leadership team back together to present the results of the progress. They may have questions to address before sharing the updates with the employees.

Next, share an update with your employees on the progress made towards the goals. You do not have to wait until progress is made on each initiative to share updates with your employees. Recall that communication is key. In fact, it's better to create a consistent cadence of sharing updates so that your employees see this is top of mind for your organization and one which you have ranked with high importance.

You Didn't Win – What Now?

The possibility of not winning recognition is a concern that sometimes keeps leaders from applying for a workplace award. Focusing time and resources to see if you get recognized is a concentrated effort. Of course, you would like to see a positive outcome.

Think back to when this journey first began. What did you identify as your WHY? Why were you applying for the award? What results were you hoping to achieve?

One of the most important actions you can take is to remind your employees of your WHY. They are going to naturally be disappointed if your organization did not make the list. This is why it's so important for organizational leaders to reinforce why this process is in place.

It is equally important to remind employees of your commitment to review their feedback from the engagement survey and share the findings with your organization. Do not hide behind the data or skew the information. Be honest and upfront with your employees about what you have learned and what you have planned for next steps towards improvement. Your employees will respect and trust your leadership and guidance.

Do you see how you have already received valuable information about your employees? If you get recognized as one of the top organizations for the award which you applied to receive, that's great. If not, look at all the data you have about your employees and make intentional choices as well as a plan to make positive changes.

More Than a Trophy

Becoming an award-winning workplace is not about the award itself. That statement may surprise you considering we are discussing how to become an award-winning workplace. Earning the award is great and, after all that hard work, it may be what you are hoping for.

However, what it is really about is what you have learned about your employees throughout the journey. This process is setting you up to listen to your employees, learn their feedback, and act through responding and goal setting. You will see your employees more engaged simply by asking them for their thoughts and opinions. You may even get improvement ideas that you had not even thought of simply by asking.

It's more than a trophy.

Whatever your WHY may be, you started on this journey because you wanted to strive for improvement with your organization. You wanted to hear how your employees feel about working for you, what they think about your leadership team, how effective they see your communication is, why they selected you as an employer, and what it takes to retain them with your company. That is more valuable than any trophy you will put on your shelf.

Angie Redmon

Angie Redmon has invested more than two decades learning what makes good companies great, and it always comes back to the same thing: Companies who care about their people as much as they care about their bottom line are more likely to recruit and retain outstanding employees. Through her dedication to workplace culture and employee engagement, Angie has developed and led HR teams with multiple companies in diverse industries.

Now, Angie is the President and Founder of striveHR, LLC, an organization focused on guiding aspirational companies through the process of pursuing a best workplace distinction. She channels her work into helping organizations develop their people strategies and guiding HR professionals to develop in their career through her coaching and mentorship. Angie has an impressive track record of helping organizations uncover employee engagement challenges and guiding organizations to achieving an award-winning workplace culture.

Angie's passion is in helping HR professionals and business leaders to create workplaces their employees are proud of, and to empower them to contribute to the success of their organization. She believes through trust and honesty, a strong workplace culture is achievable.

Angie is a speaker and blogger, and podcast guest discussing topics such as:

- What it takes to be an award-winning workplace
- Why you should care about being an award-winning workplace
- You applied for an award, but now what
- Why HR departments need a business coach

Angie earned a Bachelor of Science in Organizational Leadership from IUPUI and holds a Certificate in Human Resources Management. She is proud of her SHRM-SCP and PHR, as well as her certification as an Employee Engagement Specialist from Top Workplaces. Angie lives near Indianapolis, IN with her husband and two children.

Connect with Angie Redmon:

LinkedIn: https://www.linkedin.com/in/angieredmonawardwinningworkplaceadvisorandhrcoach

Website: https://strivehr.net

Facebook: https://www.facebook.com/striveHR

Email: angie@strivehr.net

4.

HR's Role in Company Culture

Kristie Dierig | Founder, CEO of Ever Spark, LLC

It was mind-blowing the first time I saw it!

While attending the McLean Signature Conference in September 2019, I had the opportunity to hear Ms. Dessalen Wood, Chief People Officer of Thought Exchange. She presented on the topic of Performance Management.

She started asking us basic questions like, "What do you need to give your best at work?" With a thick black marker in hand, she jotted down the answers on the flip chart onstage as we shouted them. "Clarity, Decisiveness, Encouragement, Trust, Autonomy..." We named the typical things that would describe great work environments.

> *Now, the following twenty items are examples of what was shared in the session. Actual items are not available for recollection.*

Then she asked us to pull out the twenty cards from the manila envelopes at our table. Each one had a word or phrase that described a working relationship, many of which we had already called out.

"Pick these five cards," she said, "and turn the rest face down. Fair Salary, Clarity, Specificity, Good Boss, Good teammates." Then she asked, "What percent of your best would you give if these were the only things you received from your Job?" A couple of people shouted "30%" or "40%." The rest of us maybe mumbled to ourselves or thought of a number in our heads, slowly following along with where this was going.

The next five cards were "Autonomy, Challenge, Purpose, Incentives, Rewards" with the same question – "What percent of our best would we give if we received these items?" Our percentages went a little higher.

Finally, we turned over the ten remaining cards: "Learning & Growth, Impact, Inspirational Leadership, Meaningful Work, Community Impact, Healthy Conflict Management, Great Culture, Personalized services, etc..." and instantly we reach 100%. Even before the exercise is complete, we understand the point she's making.

I sat there with my previous traditional HR paradigms of Performance and Talent Management totally obliterated! How did I not see this before? How has HR not seen this before? How have businesses been able to control these levers at all times and yet still determine pay and promotion based on a person's ability to operate in the work environments that we set for them? How do I go back to work after seeing this?! I had so many questions!!

Working for a large, global corporation at the time, I attempted to bring this insight back into our Talent Management team; but I quickly realized the idea was broader than performance management. The traditional Performance Management train (i.e., work plan agreement, quarterly and annual reviews, and then a five-point rating scale to influence range of pay) had long ago left the station and wasn't coming back. Likewise, it was far too complicated to track and influence the twenty vectors that Ms. Wood identified as characteristics of an ideal environment because there wasn't one person fully responsible for those elements, and measuring each of them would be complicated and perhaps subjective.

However, the more time I spent thinking about it, I realized there were some common elements across all these items-elements that are often a product of the role HR plays, or can play, within the organization.

And then the lightbulb really went off!

Is HR 100% responsible for the workplace environment?

Think about it!

HR sets Policy.

HR runs the Recruiting process.

HR runs internal job postings and career moves.

HR runs Manager and Leadership training programs.

HR manages people transitions (hire, leave of absence, issue resolution, separation)

HR runs Employee Engagement surveys.

HR runs Compensation.

They are nearly 100% responsible for the overall Employee Experience.

By definition, HR builds, delivers, and maintains policies and programs that indicate acceptable and unacceptable behavior in the workplace. Likewise, in the spirit of what Ms. Wood has challenged us to consider, if HR isn't looking at this holistically, they might be totally missing the mark.

The Big Idea

For decades now, HR has perfected the steps around putting processes and compliance procedures in place. HR is really good at this, as they are designed to be because documentation, tracking, and compliance are key for accountability and legal requirements in the workplace. Yet, how often does HR think about how their actions contribute to the desired Company Culture? And why are these factors missing in the first place?

Before we go there, let's look at some examples of what we do today and why we do it.

I Had to Learn the Hard Way

As a junior HR Business Partner, I was eager and well intended, but quickly learned it was more than managing processes and tracking compliance. There was one occasion where an employee's boyfriend passed away suddenly. I consulted with her and her manager to explain she had 3 days of bereavement and had requested an extra week off. I put her data in the system and noted when her return to work date was. I thought my job was done.

However, a week later she called to chat and ask some follow-up questions. It was a good conversation, but I could tell she was still sad and working through her grief. I was also thinking about her return to work date. So, before we hung up I asked "By when do you think you'll be back to work?..." To me, it was an innocent question and one that I thought was uniquely my job. Man – did I learn quickly it was the WRONG thing to say! She expressed immediate shock and dismay at my suggestion, which upon reflection did seem a bit aggressive and misplaced, so I apologized and just waited for her manager to indicate when she was ready to return. (Now – mind you – this was in my early days of being an HR Business Partner, so please give me some grace if you already learned this hard lesson! This was also pre-pandemic...so things were different then!)

But I also wondered – isn't that my job? If that's our policy, aren't I the one who is supposed to know the policy and enforce it? Didn't she expect the question was coming? What type of Culture did I create in doing this?

Performance Improvement Plans

I also had a friend who experienced a painful Performance Improvement Plan (PIP). He was a high performing, highly committed employee working in a job that was a perfect fit for him and his unique talents. However, with several department reorganizations and 3 bosses in 12 months later, he was struggling to connect with his team and the work. On top of that, there were some challenges at home that needed his attention too. It was becoming a lot to manage.

As the year progressed, the stress was starting to take its toll. He was still committed as ever, but found it hard to concentrate at work. He felt less creative, less responsive, and less connected to the work he knew he was capable of delivering. He reached out to his manager for help, but didn't get much of a response. He used EAP and it didn't seem to help either.

Finally, during a regular 1-to-1 with his manager, he arrived prepared to demonstrate the latest progress on his projects, without asking for additional help. Surprisingly, he found himself face-to-face with HR. He was presented with a Performance Improvement Plan – the first in his career! Suffice it to say it did not entirely help.

He remained committed and worked hard to meet the expectations of the PIP. However, two weeks before the agreed deadline, his manager told him it's not working out and his role was going to be eliminated. So, he had to go to HR to find another role within the company, or be let go.

As an HR Professional, I understand there is a purpose to a PIP, as accountability and documentation are needed to manage employees who are not performing the expected job duties. However, how many times are good employees lost because of a failure to use the right tools based on the situation and/or apply solutions that actually build the employee up? What type of Culture was being created when HR delivered this PIP and told the employee their job is eliminated 2 weeks before the documented deadline?

Performance Management

"I am so excited! My manager and I get to review my results from the past year!"... said no employee, ever.

Yes, it is true that employees need goals, strategies, and clear accountability to do their job and do it in support of company objectives. Many companies continue to run these programs with great success. However, when it becomes something employees and managers dread, then perhaps there's a different way to do it.

If you set a goal to climb Mt. Everest, and get 90% of the way there, do you say "Aw shucks! Missed expectations. Fail!" No – you celebrate all that you did to prepare, train, and actually take the climb. Despite being 10% short of your goal, you celebrate because you did the work, you learned along the way, and you gained an amazing experience. The experience and the journey is the memory you hold on to and the story you tell time and time again.

Why can't work be like this? Future thinkers and innovators are avidly writing about this now. The cover page of SHRM's HR Manager magazine, Spring 2023 says "Performance Reviews are Broken."[1] Perhaps many HR Professionals have read or heard about new ways to manage performance. So, why do we keep running the same process, year after year? Are we even aware of the Culture we're creating by keeping this process running, despite the resistance?

Reflection

This is a pivotal time for HR. HR professionals are capable, committed, and keenly aware of the changes happening...and yet are feeling overwhelmed and burnt out. In fact, HR Leaders are among the most likely to leave their employer, according to the HR Executive report from March 2023.[2] They're buried in the weight of the post-pandemic, talent-power-shifting, cultural and social changes, generationally-charged workforce in addition to delivering the standard, compliant and operationally sound programs. There's a lot going on! If HR is feeling all of this and considering leaving, then who will remain to impact culture?

Is HR even in a position to do it? Did you know there's an official category of Human Resources funny on TikTok?[3] Why is it that HR seems to be the butt of jokes when it comes to work? Recall Toby in the US sitcom "The Office." Even HR Professionals would laugh, right? Because we can all relate in some way.

So, in the face of huge workloads, burnout, attrition, and comedic expectations, this area is ripe for transformation. So, how will they get ahead and/or who can help them think differently in order to face these insurmountable challenges? Speakers from stages or thinkers from pages with eye-opening examples, like Ms. Dessalen Wood, can only take us so far. It is up to each of us to recognize that the way we have been doing things can no longer be the plan for the future and that NOW is the time to change.

We Simply Cannot Stay the Course

In 2023, we have come to a point where the risk of continuing to do what we do is no longer sustainable and needs to change. Here are what I'll call the "5 Risks of Staying the Course":

1. <u>HR defines a narrow scope of Impact on Culture</u> – It is true that HR is responsible for Culture and that birthdays, service anniversaries, rewards, community events, team building, and personal life milestones are activities that often fall under the HR umbrella. However, Culture is also the outcome of well-designed organizations that identify and incentivize desired behaviors and align to business results. HR is also an incredible influencer of Culture, in nearly everything they touch! So, HR can afford to have a broader view of their impact on Culture.

2. <u>HR focuses on the Individual</u> – HR programs such as Performance Management, Compensation, Training, and Employee Relations focus on the individual and how they operate within the workplace. Yet, the missed opportunity is in measuring organizational health, as captured by Organizational Design effectiveness, Cultural Health, Team dynamics, manager performance, innovation health, and psychological safety, to name a few. As demonstrated by Ms. Wood's exercise, employees will give more when they are set-up in environments that are designed to request their

best.

3. <u>HR focuses on Process Execution</u> – HR teams may build and execute programs, policies, and processes to deliver the necessary compliance steps and documentation, but may miss the opportunity to deliver a meaningful experience or any other business important objectives. Designing solutions that take into account multiple requirements (compliance, process, experience, business objectives, automation, etc...) will achieve far-greater results.

4. <u>HR delivers traditional programs</u> – Delivering the same traditional programs such as performance management, PIPs, annual compensation, traditional training programs etc...will limit what's possible and what's needed in the next five years. Now is the time to innovate, transform, automate, and maybe even prune what and how we do it. To stay the course and continue delivering the same year-upon-year will further divide the solution from the need.

5. <u>HR assumes that IT will take care of the techie-stuff</u> – While it is true, IT departments do hold key roles in the design and delivery of technology and software, the rapid changes in today's workplace are happening faster than what two departments can keep pace with. The future requires all levels of HR to have a deeper understanding of how technology works and how to use it to transform workplace processes and experiences. The more democratized this knowledge is, the better the two departments will be able to

collaborate and the faster the innovative ideas will occur.

How to Flip the Script

So, if HR is to move beyond processes and compliance tracking, where do they begin? Here are five areas to consider:

1. <u>Move beyond the "Fun" Culture Programs</u>. Add capacity by shifting work to an employee-led social committee. HR should only do Programs and onsite events that intentionally build on the Business Objectives and Culture. Does your office also need a football BBQ and spring picnic?! Sure thing! Just ask other employees to do it. This would give HR space to build the strategic impact of their programs and/or even how a football BBQ can help drive the Business objectives.

2. <u>Build programs that design for and measure Organizational and Managerial effectiveness</u>. Balance the Individual with the Organizational focus and look for mutual inclusivity. Start by taking Ms. Dessalen Wood's model to heart and measure those twenty factors on a regular basis. Then, equip managers and leaders with the policies, tools, and programs to deliver them.

3. <u>Lead with a Human-centered, Experience-based Approach</u>. Intentionally build a human-based design in

the most-used products and programs to make meaningful experiences. Meaningful experiences can look like something personal, purposeful (life-giving, relief-giving, love-sharing...), simple, kind, or thoughtful. Any time we think about intentionally designing the Human experience in the policies and programs we deliver, the better our impact on company culture will be.

4. <u>Explore alternate methods of delivering Traditional Programs</u>. Ask yourself: What is the root problem we're trying to solve with this program?

   ○ Is this program a typical HR "out of the box" solution or has it been designed to uniquely support our company?
   ○ What about this program aligns with our business objectives and company purpose? Which of these can we enhance or remove?
   ○ How do we measure the Value this program brings? How can we set-up sustainable ways of measuring value and integrating it into our Business Strategies?
   ○ What is the desired Employee Experience and how can I capture the necessary information while also personalizing, streamlining, or even delighting them as well?
   ○ Are there any unintended consequences of our activities that go against desired culture and business objectives?

5. Transform, Automate, and Analyze everywhere you can. Similar to how Marketing changed since 2000 in the digital age, so now is true for HR. The more we can innovate, automate, and digitize – the more data we have. The more data we have, the more knowledge we gain. Therefore, the more value we can create. There will be new frontiers in measuring productivity and value among the largest item on the Balance Sheet – people costs! Where profit margins are being squeezed, this is the next place to explore. Now is the time to invest, innovate, and build tools for new insights for the next wave of measured value and change.

6. Consider the Design of your HR Team. If your HR department is buried under the weight of all that's expected right now, then it's time for a new model. Adding more hours to the day is not an option and solving the problems in the same ways, – as Albert Einstein said – expecting different results, is the definition of insanity. A new approach is the solution. Here are a few ideas to get started:

   ○ Maintain the current HR team but make clear distinctions between the different areas (e.g. Operations, Service Delivery, and Business Partnership). Consider also adding an Employee Experience role/team and/or an Innovation role/team.

   ○ Think strategically about the work of HR for now and the future. Consider:

- What work does my internal HR staff need to do versus what can be outsourced?
- What work among my staff adds the most value, and what can be automated?
- Which part of our employee experiences need a human touch, versus others that just need a process/form/document?
- Where are our business strategies/employee expectations/competitor practices/industry trends headed in the next 5 years and what do I need to proactively plan for?

○ Build a Service Delivery mindset around your HR Products and Programs, with things like employee listening, satisfaction, innovation pipeline, usage, impact, and value. Then build an employee-centered, continuous improvement, value driven set of activities around each product, to ensure continued results and overall success.

○ Institute key metrics around the most impactful activities, operationalize, and track diligently. (For example, measure "Retention Fit" for a new person in a role vs. "Time to Fill" in applicant tracking.) Fully integrate these metrics into the business scorecards and success criteria.

○ Upskill your HR team in the spirit of systemic thinking, design thinking, employee experience, creative problem-solving, and organization design.

Don't Follow the Rules Out the Window

All this being said – let's not stop doing what we do best: taking care of people and ensuring a safe and lawful workplace. The key responsibilities of HR are still very important to overall company operations. There are still many things in the workplace that are incredibly important to maintain in this area and HR is responsible for much of it.

Let's also keep bringing a more human spirit to work. The pandemic taught us we are more than just "work people" and "home people" – we are both all day long. It also taught us that even though we are extremely resilient, we are also fragile, and still living in a world that carries heartbreak and trauma. There is no better department than HR to bring awareness, education, and policies that allow people to be human AND be great employees, too!

Let's keep investing in Managers and Leaders. Manager and Leaders' abilities to lead people through ambiguity and change, and do so with a servant heart, is critical to business success in today's marketplace. HR is responsible, and incredibly capable, in equipping their leaders to do this and do it well. Our Managers, Leaders, and Employees, need us now more than ever!

Lastly, let's not assume that everything we are doing today is ancient and archaic. Innovation and Digital Transformation are not urgent answers for everyone, nor the magic wand that makes everything better. There are many businesses who are just fine operating using traditional models, simple spreadsheets, and predictable HR programs and processes. The best solution is to remain aware and be in a position of change readiness so that when it's time to change, you are ready.

In Closing

It is an exciting time to be in HR! The cookie-cutter approach is no longer enough and the options for change are abundant. Faced with dramatic change, leaders and employees need HR more than ever. The invitation is simply this – think one step beyond the traditional ways and think about the experience it will bring for the humans who will use it.

HR Professionals are the most compassionate, caring, and empathetic people I know and therefore, the most capable people to answer the call! With the right paradigms, structures, skills, and tools, I am confident we will evolve our programs and make intentional impacts on company cultures. I look forward to the day when everyone is able to give their best because the workplace conditions support, encourage, and even celebrate their best efforts!

Notes

1. "HR Magazine: Spring 2023." SHRM, 27 Apr. 2023, www.shrm.org/hr-today/news/hr-magazine/spring-2023/Pages/default.aspx.

2. Kawamoto, Dawn. "Burnout for HR Leaders Isn't Getting Any Better. What Can Be Done?" HR Executive, 13 Mar. 2023, hrexecutive.com/burnout-for-hr-leaders-isnt-getting-any-better-what-can-be-done/.

3. "Human Resources Funny | Tiktok Search." TikTok, www.tiktok.com/discover/human-resources-funny?lang=en. Accessed 24 May 2023.

Kristie Dierig

Kristie Dierig is the founder and CEO of Ever Spark, LLC, a boutique consulting firm focused on helping companies build workplace experiences, practices, and processes relevant for the 21st-century business.

Kristie started Ever Spark with a passion to help her fellow HR professionals in upskilling and transforming the way they deliver products and services after seeing the dramatic changes in IT and recognizing the parallels between them.

She started her career studying Industrial Engineering at the University of Michigan, which led her to a full-time IT position at Procter & Gamble. While at P&G, she had the opportunity to move into HR and obtain her Masters of Human Resource Development at Xavier University. She stayed there for twenty-one years leading global programs in website and database administration, commercial analytics, career and talent development, people analytics, and finally played many key roles in the implementation of Workday for their global workforce.

Her approach is rooted in 21st-century tools such as Design Thinking, Human-centered Leadership, Innovation, Agile Culture, and continuous improvement. She also has a passion in finding the balance between what's trending versus what's relevant and most value-additive for her clients.

At Ever Spark, she delivers unique holistic solutions for businesses, teams, and individuals through fractional advisory services and consulting projects centered around organizational design and development, program effectiveness evaluations, HR technology assessment and implementation, change management, employee voice evaluations, and transformational workshops and speaking engagements underpinned by the power of people.

She's passionate about creating an exciting place to work that entices today's generation, and generations to come.

Kristie is also an active facilitator at the Xavier Leadership Center, providing inspiration and education to business leaders in Greater Cincinnati in the areas of Management Essentials, Decision Making, and Customer Experience.

Kristie is a proud Polish-Italian native of Detroit, now Northern Kentucky resident, with a spouse and two amazing boys. She loves her Greater Cincinnati community and supports it through volunteering, board membership, and other philanthropic activities. She also enjoys connecting with her athletic roots through rowing, running, weight lifting, and yoga.

Kristie's ideas and inspirations can be found on her website (ever-spark.com), LinkedIn, Speaking Engagements, or Podcasts found at:

- Mindability – Future Speak (Sam Eaton)
- Mental Health for Leaders (Lindsay Recknell)
- Disrupt HR (Cincinnati 2014)

Connect with Kristie Dierig:

LinkedIn: http://www.linkedin.com/in/kristiedierig

Website: http://www.ever-spark.com

5.

Tools to Retain Talent and Make Culture Relevant

Melanie Booher | Culture Coach

The big day was here.

I was feeling thrilled, a little nervous, and my palms were getting a bit sweaty. Excitement. More nervousness. I could feel my heart beating faster than usual. I had prepared intently – and while I could speak about culture in my sleep...this time was going to be different.

I was veering away from my typical culture presentation, creating a new technology and gamification angle. And I certainly do not consider myself a technology or gamification guru! It was a bit of a gamble – but one that I was willing to take. I was choosing to take my life's passion and cast a wider net. An opportunity for bigger impact. An opportunity to make a ripple of good.

As I entered the conference room, I was secretly just hoping that a few inquisitive souls had signed up for my session. Goodness, please don't let the room be empty!

To my surprise, the room was filling up quickly. Even the annoying-to-get-to-middle seats and eager-beaver front-row seats were taken. The event planner leaned over to me and said, "This is amazing – you have filled the room! We are going to have to close the doors because the Fire Marshall is really strict about avoiding overcrowding!" She nicely told the attendees who were standing around mingling that they would have to find a seat, and sit on the floor if needed. Then, she closed the door.

Full. Completely full. I was brimming with pride – and I hadn't done a darn thing yet!

This was proof.

Proof that people are excited to find new methods, tools, and/or ideas to move culture forward at their companies. Proof that prior talks about culture were good, but this was going to be great. Proof that leaders are ready to try new things to instill a great workplace culture. Proof that trusting our gut isn't a good culture strategy. Proof that doing the same thing over and over again isn't yielding the desired results.

Oh yes, it's time for a change.

For years, I've been on a quest to make the world better one workspace at a time – amplifying workplaces with culture work. Now, I believe that I have found the true multiplier – gamification! I look forward to teaching you more about this fun and unique approach to creating great workplace culture. Let's explore this together. Game on!

Culture Matters

There's no denying that culture is a hot topic in the workplace. As we have more and more culture conversations, my consulting team repeatedly hears the need for an improvement in workplace culture. Layer in societal challenges (like pandemics, societal unrest, political upheaval, remote work, burnout, and more!) and workplace culture becomes even more critical to business success.

Do challenging times impact culture? Absolutely- before, during, and after the onset of those challenging times. Culture never stays the same. It's always changing. Now, more than ever, culture is under the microscope.

The purpose of this chapter is quite simple: to help leaders understand the importance of their most important asset – their people. Organizations must rally their teams around aligned values and habits. Leaders need to be more intentionally focused on culture, outline a plan to improve, and utilize resources, ideas, tools, and strategic interventions (many of which can be found in this book!) to design an intentional culture strategy of your own.

Company culture is often thought of as the values and behaviors that are displayed within an organization. These values and behaviors determine the ways things get done. Good news: every company has a culture. Bad news: most leaders think they can create a best-in-class culture by trusting their gut and rarely create a strategic plan to help guide them in the creation and cultivation of the type they desire.

NEWS FLASH: an amazing culture takes intentional effort (with ongoing leadership attention) and develops gradually over time. There's no magic wand.

Assess your organizational culture and customize a culture strategy with an ongoing purpose that ensures your people matter – just as much (maybe even more!) as your financial statement. When done correctly, your people can drive those financial forecasts through the roof. My vision has always been: "When people matter, companies THRIVE!" And ongoing business success follows those who adopt this people-first vision.

There is no one way to do culture correctly. There are a variety of ways that culture can be brought to life within your organization. Whether you choose a manual process or going digital – the important piece is that you are being intentional, have a plan, working culture into habits, and having some fun along the way. In order for culture to stick, we must be a SAP (it needs to be **Strategic**, we hold people **Accountable**, and we always maintain a **People-centric** lens). This is the secret to ensuring culture is relative, engaging, and actionable!

Ideas to Move Culture Forward

We can move, and should, be moving culture forward in a myriad of ways:

- Holding meaningful culture conversations
- Gamifying leadership discussions (*Cards for Culture*)
- Utilizing a creative yet organized plan to provide structure (the THRIVE™ Model)
- Working it into processes with the company (the power of habit)
- Having some fun along the way (ex. adding culture challenges to the mix!)

Why gamify?

Gamification is a new realm, loosely identified as the process of applying game mechanics and elements to non-game activities in order to engage and motivate people. Ask just about anyone – and they would rather play a game than work. So the golden nugget here is that we are combining these two elements (games/work) and having great success with it! Gamification can be a powerful tool for driving better workplace culture, as it can help to:

- Increase employee engagement and motivation
- Improve communication and collaboration

- Promote learning and development
- Drive productivity among teammates
- Build a sense of community and belonging
- Reinforce company values

Currently, my team is working on a variety of ways to gamify. In order to appeal to a wide variety of users, we have options that are both in-person-friendly (like decks of cards) and remote-friendly (like surveys, Culture Challenges, and our Culture Community!)

Of course, the digital gaming world is continually changing – it's a new and exciting frontier. I'm certain by the time this book is published, we will have changed and improved things a few times. Everyone must embrace change and roll with the punches.

Think of the old Chinese proverb – "When's the best time to plant a tree? Twenty years ago." Then, you'd already have shade. The second best time to plant a tree is now! So, we apply that to our gamifying – when's the best time to gamify? Yesterday. However, the second best time is now!

Traditional Gaming Options

First, we offer *Cards for Culture*, which is our alpha product (a deck of physical cards) that got the whole thing started. Modeled after popular games like Cards Against Humanity or Apples to Apples, *Cards for Culture* was created to help define the desired culture within a company or organization and get everyone on the same page. This business tool brings to life and gamifies the process of discussing company values, defining the behaviors that drive those values, and then brainstorming ways to bring the culture to life with increased visibility and process-driven habits.

Organizations can play the game themselves, utilize a business coach, or engage one of our PEOPLEfirst Culture Coaches to facilitate the game – choose whichever option makes the most sense for you and your organization. To help leaders understand how the tool is best utilized, we have a directions page that comes with the game, a video on YouTube, an e-learning option, and a (soon-to-be-offered) certification for leaders to become Certified Culture Champions. Certified Culture Champions will learn how to build a strong foundation for companies. Let's look at it using a strong oak tree as an example: there are two kinds of employees – oaks or saplings. Oak trees are fully rooted and loyal while saplings, or newbies, are easily transplanted. My PEOPLEfirst team is nurturing and creating oak trees! Therefore, we refer to them as such – OAKS. Our Advisors for Keys to Success.

Building off of *Cards for Culture*, we also created our *Cards for Culture – Recruitment Edition.* This is a micro-deck which can be utilized during the recruitment process. Because it's a micro-deck, it is quick and more digestible. This makes it more fun, engaging, and value-driven.

Imagine you sit down with a candidate and ask them to pick a few cards that are important to them. What they pick (and what they don't) are very telling. Dig in with questions located on the back of each card (and tied to that value!) in order to learn more.

What is the objective of using *Cards for Culture*? To assess the candidate's fit by bringing forward key values and utilizing the corresponding questions. You should be looking for a candidate that is a culture add, meaning those who have similar values but also bring some unique traits to the table by way of diversity. Add something to our culture! Don't be culture drains/negatives! Answers will be unique to each organization, aligning with the Keys to Success and Defining Behaviors that were determined from the *Cards for Culture* game.

What a unique, fun, and value-driven approach to ensure you are talking to the right people.

Digital Gaming Options

In today's tech savvy world – there has been a big push for digital options. Therefore, we have created a new platform where companies can engage their team through Culture Challenges.

We utilize an app to get your team signed up, into a challenge, and participating. While each Challenge may be tailored and unique, often core elements surface (like our Keys to Success: Integrity, Communication, Service, and Innovation).

A culture challenge helps keep your Keys to Success (values) top of mind. To make things fun and engaging, we utilize:

- Daily Inspirations: quotes to motivate and inspire your team
- Wall-of-Wins: positive contributions from teammates that are shared among the team (complete with high fives for additional team engagement)
- Gratefulness & Personal Journaling: opportunities to create a gratefulness habit to spur a positive mindset among your team and also personal reflections that get the team thinking of their intentional culture habits
- Daily Intention: reminders of what culture means to your organization, to entrench into our common language so that it's "just how we do business around here!"
- Coaches Corner: videos and micro-lessons provided from our Culture Coaches or your own leadership team (if desired)
- Weekly Challenges: opportunities to dig deeper into our lessons and habits
- Leaderboard: display that creates competitive spirit and show points/ranking for prizes

At the end of our Culture Challenges, we hold a Recognition Ceremony to learn more about the team's culture wins throughout the event. We look for trends in the data, view statistics to see levels of engagement, and celebrate those who participated with verbal praise and prizes.

Culture Challenges are a great way to engage remote teammates and bring them into the fold with the entire team. While participation is not mandatory, we see growing positive trends. Gamification fosters a subtle shift from being something the team feels they "have to do" into something they "want to do"! And that's a culture win for everyone!

Why create challenges?

There are many reasons why creating digital culture challenges can be a great way to create fun and engagement around workplace culture. Companies are keeping up with technology trends and also trying to reach teammates across the globe – so going digital can make this an easier task. Here are a few reasons why you might consider doing this also:

- To build relationships and camaraderie. When employees work together to complete a challenge, they have to communicate and collaborate with each other. Because this leads to building good relationships and creating camaraderie, a more positive and productive work environment is achievable.

- To break up the monotony of work. A little bit of fun and excitement can go a long way in making work and the workday more enjoyable.
- To promote learning and development. Culture challenges can be a great way to learn new things and develop new skills. When employees are challenged to learn something new, they are more likely to retain the information.
- To support and encourage a positive mindset. We know that a positive mindset plus gamification equals results – and that's what we are going for.
- Culture challenges can be a great way to reinforce company values. When employees are challenged to do things that align with the company's values, they are more likely to internalize those values.

This is a new frontier – we have not seen the digital era encompassing culture initiatives until now! Many CEOs have built their own ideas of a good culture on the backs of happy hours and ping-pong tables. We all know that we can do better! Gamifying helps with just that. As we learn more and more about how to make these most successful, fun, and engaging – we've discovered a few tips for creating culture challenges:

- Make sure the challenges are relevant to your company's culture. The challenges should be something that your employees will be interested in and that will align with your company's values.
- Make the challenges achievable. The challenges should

require some effort from participants, but they should also be able to be completed successfully. If the challenges are too difficult, employees will get discouraged and give up.

- Make the challenges fun. The challenges should be something that employees will enjoy doing. If the challenges are not fun, employees will not be motivated to participate.
- Be flexible and willing to adapt the game as needed.
- Get leader buy-in and encourage leaders to participate and lead by example. The challenges will be better accepted by all when this happens!
- Reward those participating in the challenges. Rewards can be anything from small prizes (gift cards) to recognition from management. Get creative! And be certain the rewards are ones that your team is excited to receive!

Our consulting team at PEOPLEfirst would love to support organizations who want to drive culture forward in a unique way. We know that when companies follow these tips, their culture challenges are fun and engaging. That's what you want! The challenges help build relationships, break up the monotony of work, promote learning and development, encourage a positive mindset, and reinforce company values. All while also promoting retention, performance, and overall company success.

More Ideas to Gamify

There are many different ways to gamify company culture. We've really just uncovered the tip of the iceberg. In fact, hearing some of these ideas might spur creative thoughts of your own – that's great! Keep the creative juices flowing. Think of ways that you can incorporate fun, games, prizes, points, or other elements of positive reinforcement to create continued excitement and engagement within your team.

Utilize the THRIVE™ Model

This is a great tool to support companies as they make sense of all the things needed in order to build a strong foundation and grow from that foundation. From roots to branches, we are reviewing processes and practices that make our culture stronger. People Operations/Human Resources support this journey, as they are the processes that we create.

Gamification should be used in conjunction with other initiatives to improve company culture. For example, we recommend supplementing gamification as we bring it to life with the THRIVE™ Model. Our THRIVE™ Model is what I recommend for creating your written culture plan. Choose which elements your company needs and be intentional in your efforts. You may download a free copy of this culture plan at thrivewithmb.com or choosepeoplefirst.com. There are many different options to build a foundation of processes infused with culture success and then level-up (grow!).

THRIVE™ (Branches):
Build a Great Workplace

Branches represent growth opportunities within an organization. Focused energy yields culture change and growth over time.

When people matter, companies THRIVE!

TALENT MATTERS

Hybrid Workforce, Talent Management System, Recruitment Partnerships, Applicant Tracking System, Behavior-Based Interviews, Referral Program, Stellar On-Boarding Process

HEALTH OF BUSINESS MATTERS

Culture Deck, Atmosphere & Workspace, Developmental Training, Engaged in Personal Life, Inclusive Community, Holistic Wellness Plan

RETENTION MATTERS

Above and Beyond Benefits, Market-Leading Comp, Meaningful Appreciation, Owner-Minded, Engagement Committee

IMPROVEMENT MATTERS

Technology (HRIS) Driven, Digital Processes, Coaching Culture, Strong Partnerships, Safety Culture & Committee, Stay Interview and Surveys

VISION MATTERS

Lived Values & Behaviors (Cards for Culture), Values Proposition, Customized Communication Plan, Internal Branding, 3rd Party/Culture Coach

ENGAGEMENT MATTERS

Personality Still Matters, Inspiring Leaders (Develop Others), Team Developed Goals, Succession Plan, Embedded Mentors, Behavior Based Coaching

The THRIVE© Model is a heatmap to assess gaps and create a Culture Plan. These are the value-based habits that our organization's conscious culture is built upon.

Roots are a foundation, a source of strength.
Weeding as we go, we create baseline success.
Start small and grow from there.

When people matter, companies THRIVE!

TALENT MATTERS

Traditional Workforce, Defined Hiring Process, In-House Recruitment,
Application/Offer Letter, Basic On-Boarding Checklist

HEALTH OF BUSINESS MATTERS

Handbook, Required Postings/Training, Job Descriptions, I-9 Process Created,
Emergency Contact Form, DE&I Awareness/Training, EAP

RETENTION MATTERS

Basic Benefits, Competitive Wages, Rewards & Recognition, Team-Minded,
Fun Events

IMPROVEMENT MATTERS

Personnel Files, Record Retention, Performance Reviews, "Do It All" Mentality,
Basic Safety Plan, Exit Interview

VISION MATTERS

Define Values & Behaviors (Cards for Culture), Understand the WHY, Open-
Door Communication, External Branding, Office Manager/ HR

ENGAGEMENT MATTERS

Personality Matters, Involved Leader (Develop Self), Management Developed
Goals. Org Structure, Development Opportunities

The THRIVE© Model is a heatmap to assess gaps and
create a Culture Plan. These are the value-based habits
that our organization's conscious culture is built upon.

Join less than 10% of companies that actually plan for their culture. We help leaders do more than just trust their gut. Create a plan, garner alignment so that everyone is on the same page, make continual improvements, and apply the power of habit. You will see the results in morale, productivity, turnover and more. Good news: it will generate a competitive advantage and ensure a resilient legacy. Bonus, this tool is FREE. You can find it on our website and/or send us an email.

Play Cards for Culture

I've mentioned this before – but it's pretty amazing so that calls for a repeat (making sure you are paying attention!) If you are looking for a new idea for alignment and progress: play Cards for Culture: The Business Edition. Think Apples to Apples (or Cards Against Humanity) with a culture vibe. This revolutionary game literally places company culture in your own hands through three different decks of cards. Even if you already have Vision & Values noted within your organization, most employees can't reiterate them. We fix that through habit formation!

Gather your top leaders, a facilitator, and set aside some time to determine your Keys for Success, Defining Behaviors, and Habits. Gamifying culture makes it memorable and fun. Bonus: amazing discussions, clarity and alignment will follow.

Join our Culture Community Events

Created for Conscious Culture Leaders who share ideas to build culture in a positive way and know it takes ongoing and intentional effort to drive culture success. Like the Culture Challenges, we have embedded similar areas of focus, which means this is also a good way to see how the Culture Challenges might work for your company on a macro-level with other culture leaders.

We share ideas, learn from each other, provide Coaches Corners, Weekly Challenges, Wall-of-Wins, Daily Inspiration, virtual high fives, and more. Currently, we are holding these on a quarterly basis so that we can award prizes and look at data trends for engagement. We'd love to have you join us in the Culture Community Event. What better way than surrounding yourself with others who believe in its importance too! You can join in the fun! Here is a link where you can join: culture.challengecreator.com/community. (If that doesn't work for some reason, connect with me on LinkedIn and I will make sure to get you connected!)

Additional gamification ideas may include:

- Using leaderboards to track employee performance
- Create a company-wide leaderboard. This could track things like sales, customer satisfaction, or employee engagement. Employees can compete against each

other to see who can reach the top of the leaderboard.

- Utilize challenges that keep culture top of mind, build community, encourage positive mindset, and offer rewards (ex. Our Culture Challenge does this!)
- Offer rewards for completing tasks or goals. These rewards could be anything from gift cards to paid time off.
- Create games, scavenger hunts, or quests that encourage employees to collaborate. These could be related to learning a new skill or completing a project within a certain time frame.
- Offering badges and rewards for completing tasks or as a simple form of positive recognition (we do this in our Culture Challenges App).

Additional Tools & Tips

If gamification isn't an option, sometimes it can be engaging to your team to offer new ideas, tools, and other digital solutions to change things up and keep your workplace culture feeling good and innovating where possible.

Here are some additional ideas that I recommend for improvement:

- Create a virtual rewards program that allows employees to redeem points for prizes.
- Nurture relationships with cards and gifts for special

occasions, birthdays, service anniversaries, and more. We recommend *SendOutCards* as an option to simplify this process, but also keep it personalized and trackable.

- Host regular fun events and activities, give points for participation and rewards/prizes to winners – in order to increase engagement. These could be anything from team-building exercises to happy hours.
- Utilize a chatbot to provide employees with real-time feedback and support.
- Use social media to create a sense of community, provide recognition, and (when possible) foster healthy competition among employees.
- Utilize LexGo as an online community for gathering space and virtual meeting rooms, in lieu of Zoom calls. My teammates enjoy this tool because it provides the ability to socialize more like a coworking space – but online. (Let me know if you'd like an introduction to the founder! It's pretty awesome!)
- Offer employee-led Zoom training sessions and workshops.
- Create a culture of continuous improvement by encouraging employees to share ideas and best practices through Slack channels, Teams, or other messenger groups.

With a little planning and effort, gamification can be a powerful tool for driving better workplace culture. It's important to use it in a meaningful and engaging way for employees.

The popularity of gamification has brought about some new and exciting options for organizations to try. With a variety of different tools and resources available for gamification, it's important to pick ones that work for your organization.

Some popular options include:

- My Culture Challenge: a platform for helping teammates celebrate, reiterate its importance, learn through microlessons, journal, and earn points/ rewards tied to the celebration of company culture.
- Gamify.me: a platform for creating and managing gamification programs.
- Badgeville: a platform for providing badges and rewards.
- Gamify.it: a platform for creating and managing games and challenges.
- CultureWise: an app that keeps culture in the palms of employees hands and builds the habit of culture.

Gamification can be a great way to improve company culture and employee engagement. By following these tips and using the right tools, you can create a gamification program that is both effective and fun.

Wrapping It Up

We've explored a variety of ways that culture can be brought to life within your organization. Whether you choose a manual process or going digital – the important piece is that you are being intentional, have a plan, working culture into habits, and having some fun along the way. That's the secret to making it relative or sticky! Be a SAP. (Sticky. Accountable. Planned.) You got this.

In today's war for talent, a unique culture approach like gamifying ensures culture is top of mind. Companies cannot merely sit around and talk about culture – leaders must take action! If gamifying is too extreme for you – be sure to at least join the Elite 10% with a culture plan!

There's no quick and easy path to bettering workplace culture; real effort is required. The weary need not apply. Roll-up your sleeves and put in the time and the effort. Leaders cannot shy away from dedication and hard work. Difficult discussions must be made (and the positive outcomes), and plan for the results that we desire. We get what we work for – not what we wish for. Therefore, it's important to stay the course, create your plan and work it. Join us in creating a better world – one leader, one workplace, one gamified experience at a time.

Melanie Booher

Melanie Booher is passionate about workplace culture. With 20+ years of business experience, and as a certified Culture Coach – Melanie helps organizations THRIVE. She is the President at PEOPLEfirst Talent & Consulting Solutions and Influence Network Media (INM), and creator of the THRIVE™ Model, *Cards for Culture©*, and *The Culture Challenge Gamification* program.

MB helps leaders understand the importance of their most important asset (their people!) and rally to bring a unique, defined culture to life. MB helps leaders understand why we must be more intentionally focused on culture, how to create a plan for improvement, and guides leaders to design an intentional culture strategy of their own.

Conscious Culture is a collective commitment that is bigger than any one of us. We can create a pay-it-forward legacy – leaving the world a better place than we found it. One good person, one game plan, and one great work culture at a time. Join the movement – knowing that together we THRIVE™!

Her first book *Conscious Culture* launched Summer of 2021. She has co-authored 6 additional books (*Talent Fusion, Powerhouse, Leadership Fusion, Marketing Fusion, 22 Women Ultrapreneurs,* and *Sales Fusion*) which spurred her to found INM – helping others find their voice and become authors also! You can find her books on Amazon. Melanie lives outside of Cincinnati, OH with her husband and 3 children.

Connect with Melanie Booher:

LinkedIn: www.linkedin.com/in/melanie-booher

Website: https://melaniebooher.com

Buy *Cards for Culture*©: cardsforculturegame.com

6.

Inner Critics

The Key to Unlocking Potential and Shifting Culture

Tosca DiMatteo | Leadership & Career Coach, Culture Consultant, Keynote Speaker, Brand Storyteller, former Unilever, Kimberly-Clark & Univision Marketing Leader

The Case for Inner Critic Work

It's time to take back your joy, your power, and your unique leadership style.

Being a people-first leader is not for the faint of heart. Your ability to experience more fulfillment in your role as a leader will grow exponentially when you dive deeper into the work of shifting your relationships with your inner critics. Period.

If you want to make real, meaningful change as a leader, then you need to go right to the root of how culture is created. How culture is created, fundamentally, begins with how people treat each other. How people treat each other begins and ends with how people treat themselves.

The thing that's going to move the needle in the potential of your organization is your ability to get to the absolute heart of the behaviors of your employees. This means you need to understand and address the inner critics that are running around unchecked, misunderstood, or (worse yet), not seen or acknowledged in the first place.

How We Treat Ourselves is Essentially How We Treat Others

Our interaction with others is very much driven by whether or not we are clear in and about the relationship we have with ourselves. Let me give you an example from my own life that I'm not proud of, but I think makes the point.

> At the age of twenty-two, I was diagnosed with Type 1 Diabetes. Truth be told, I never received the support I needed to deal with the diagnosis on all levels.
>
> For years, I would scoff at my doctors; honestly, I was

downright rude to them. I hated going in for my appointments, and I mean hated it. I would be extremely emotional, but I didn't really understand why. I just knew that I never entered or left my appointments feeling good. In fact, I usually left in tears and with a heavy heart.

I eventually came to understand that I felt ashamed about my diagnosis and hadn't really fully accepted it either. I felt alone and, frankly, I was scared. I lived with an inner critic in my head every minute of the day. I beat myself up for having this diagnosis, and even more so, I berated myself for everything I ate. If it wasn't a piece of lettuce, it seemed, I was making the wrong decision. Living with Type 1 became yet another way I was hard on myself.

When I showed up to my appointments, I carried with me all of this unresolved history and inability to process what I was going through. I treated everyone there just the same way I was treating myself. With disdain, frustration, and hate.

I deliberately chose an example about interactions outside of the work environment. This is because compartmentalizing our humanity is how we got into the situation we are in with organizational culture. But, that's a topic for another book.

Knowing what your inner critic is telling you will provide a pretty clear understanding of how you're treating yourself.

Inner critics tell you:

- "You don't know what you're doing."
- "You don't belong here; you just got lucky."
- "They don't like you."
- "Don't speak up in the meeting – you're gonna sound stupid."
- "You're gonna fail, so don't even try it."
- "You can't afford it."

Even at the highest levels, after many career wins and business growth success stories, this is when inner critics can actually show up even more. It may sound counterintuitive, but it absolutely happens, for a multitude of reasons. Maybe the stakes feel higher, and we worry we can't keep up the momentum or we diminish our part in those achievements in the first place.

Let's be honest – we don't treat ourselves very well, especially in the context of our jobs and careers! If we haven't tended to our inner critics, they can feed us lies and therefore feed our insecurities.

If you're a part of an intentionally ignored community or non-dominant culture, the harsh messages and cruel behaviors can be amplified and multiplied exponentially. Experiences of suppression and hardship get passed down from generation to generation, including of course, racism. It shows up in many ways, and the untangling of truth, narratives and self-protection is game-changing to unlock potential. If you work with folks that are a part of these communities, I encourage curiosity into what inner critics may be present as a result of their unique and incredibly challenging experiences.

Before going any further, let's take a moment to explore what these inner critics actually are, and how they came to be.

What are Inner Critics, Exactly?

Inner critics are the messages you tell yourself that don't actually serve you – neither in the short or long term. They are a subset of the inner dialogue that many people have with themselves. While the inner monologue research varies greatly, anywhere from 30-75% of people experience this internal dialogue. I think this is vastly understated as inner critic dialog is a universal human experience.

Inner critic messages (or feelings) often come from a place deep in your past when you needed those messages to keep you safe or to help you get what you needed to survive. They can show up as self-critical, but these messages are not just about confidence. Inner critic messages can range from ideas about finances and risk taking, to blame for other people's actions, and even made up stories about what other people are thinking about you.

These messages come from your mind as a way to protect

your heart. Think about what happens when your heart is at risk. By risk here I mean: desiring and seeking acceptance, belonging, and love. One survival technique is to ignore (or stuff) the feelings of your heart and instead move into your rational, logical brain to figure things out. This creates a situation where you're relying so much on your mind, that you ignore an important and powerful tool – what your heart has to say. This is why when we're facing big decisions or are in a state of high stress, we have to remind ourselves to honor what our gut is saying – because our mind can easily hijack our whole system.

Over time, these messages can craft your behavior. They may become so embedded in fact, you may think it's who you are at your core. You may have come to believe that it's "how you think" and may have accepted negative feelings as being comfortable (it can be subconscious). But these critical voices are parts that got overdeveloped and overly loud, and those unprocessed feelings are part of what's holding you back from your full potential.

The watch out is when you take action (or inaction) because of your inner critic voice. This is because their dirty little secret is that they're liars. Here's a true story to illustrate...

> I have always been good at, and enjoyed, speaking in front of audiences. As part of my mission in the world, my desire to speak to the masses in service of helping people to think differently about what's possible has only grown further. For years I had an inner critic telling

me that it made no sense for me to go after speaking opportunities. This critic told me that "everyone" is trying to get speaking engagements, with more credibility than I, and it didn't make sense for me to even bother.

Of course, none of this was true – this was a narrative I was telling myself to prevent disappointment. The reality is that I listened to my inner critics, despite my desire to pursue speaking gigs. I'm happy to say that I've since changed my relationship with this negative nay-sayer, taken action to go after my dreams, and as a result, I have booked several paid speaking gigs!

Unfortunately, you can have several different inner critics, and they can even show up all at once. So, what about those days when they all show up? That's what I call a "bad day", and a day that requires taking really good care of yourself. Inner critics can range from being downright mean to being passive-aggressive, to acting like they are your own matter-of-fact best friend. Truth be told, if we allow ourselves the chance to feel how these voices make us feel, it can really, really hurt and cause damage for years to come.

It's not your fault that you have inner critics, in fact, it's important not to judge yourself or others for this. Inner critics are a part of being human, and as a reminder, these voices were developed at one point in our life to either protect us or assuage us of disappointment. Let me give you another example.

I was born with a visible birth defect called cleft-lip-and-palate and to protect myself from feeling hurt by other kids' cruel comments, I had a voice that told me things like "don't try to make friends with them; you don't belong." While this may have protected me from some heartbreak at an incredibly vulnerable age, I was also denying myself the chance to discover great relationships by not holding space for what could be possible. As I entered the workforce, these voices continued to keep me small and hidden in groups that I felt intimidated by. It's been my life's work to take action from another place within me, to not listen to these voices, and to eventually shift my entire relationship with narratives that were holding me back.

The world we live in today does not teach us to treat ourselves well. We are given so many messages to avoid failure at all costs. We are told it's not okay to take breaks from careers or seek out better opportunities because we might fail. The list goes on and on – and then consider how this has shown up in organizations with systems like forced ranking and scarcity mentalities. These spaces are a hotbed for inner critics to show up loud and proud.

Consider these questions:

- When you show up at work, who is really showing up there? Is it your highest self, or is it your inner critic running the show?
- When you're triggered, are you able to respond rather

than react? Does your inner critic come in and snowball the whole thing?

- When facing uncertainty of any kind, what is your go-to response?

The true bedrock and catalyst for culture change is to introduce inner critic work at EVERY. SINGLE. LEVEL. Those who have the least amount of power (in all aspects of this word), often have the heaviest load to carry. There is a compound effect for those who don't have the tools to manage their inner-world, and who also have to discern the projections of other people's inner critics. The need for self-awareness and emotional intelligence (and agility) is critical in the task of not internalizing the inner critic slime that, knowingly or not, is oozing out from others.

The greatest way that we, as leaders, can impact all the spaces we show up in is to ask ourselves: Who am I being when I show up here?

Unpacking this question and taking action accordingly, is the most powerful way that you can impact company culture.

Let me be clear in my definition of being a leader: you are a leader if you are willing to be held accountable and responsible for how you are treating yourself and others. This is regardless of if you have direct reports or not.

Shifting focus from the WHAT to the HOW

If impacting company culture is on the top of your agenda, then my counsel to you is to flip the script on how you start meetings. Often, meetings start with questions like, "Tell me about how your project progressed this past month," or "Where are we with the plan?" As a result, employees are trained to focus and be prepared with all the updates on the WHAT, WHAT, and WHAT of their jobs.

My advice is to start with questions around the how, such as:

- "How have you built internal partnerships this week?"
- "How did you engage and uplift your team members?"
- "How have your relationships with internal and external partners shifted for the better over the past month?"

My guess is that, at this moment, these questions would stop folks right in their tracks. This should tell you something. If these questions feel foreign or even obtrusive, then do we think that people are really paying attention to their how? Which means, do we think they are really paying attention to the way they are interacting with others?

Here's the other amazing benefit of flipping the script – you will likely uncover where the roadblocks are to efficiency and effectiveness in achieving your business and performance goals. Regardless of what industry or function you are in, execution relies upon the workforce's ability to collaborate and problem solve.

This is just the tip of the iceberg for how your organization can start to shift focus towards relationships and the HOW of getting work done. This can lead to conversations about what people are experiencing internally; which, again, is the heartbeat of your organization. Why? Because this is what drives behaviors. There's plenty of research on this, but this particular quote from the 2015 extensive research review, "Emotion and Decision Making", makes a potent point; "...whether we decide to pursue cooperative or competitive strategies with others depends on our beliefs about their intentions (cf. Singer & Fehr 2005), information that is often inferred from their emotions (Fessler 2007)."[1]

It's easy to start pointing at others and talk about the work THEY need to do. But, as a leader, the best and most effective way to drive change and to lead others, is to start with yourself.

Let's look at the top three things you can do as a leader to get started on inner critic work. I have seen the ripple effect that this work can have hundreds of times. So, don't discount that you can start to shift the culture on your very own team. Even better news, you can start right this very moment.

The First Three Steps: Change the Relationship with Your Inner Critic

Step 1: Deepen Your Own Inner Critic Awareness

You may have lived so long with your inner critic that you think you know it inside and out; but I promise you, there is more to learn.

> As I mentioned earlier, my inner critic would incessantly chime in about my appearance and as a result left me feeling "less than." Other times, I received direct messages that only fueled these critical voices. As a teenager, someone close to me said; "You can be anything you want, except a model." I didn't realize the influence and impact this one statement had on me from adolescence through my adult career. The impact became crystal clear on the day I saw a Sephora ad. This ad showcased a woman with a cleft-lip-and-palate as one of their models. It stopped me in my tracks!! Seeing this ad deepened my understanding of my inner critic. I truly understood, once and for all, that inner critics are liars and they don't have a clue about what's possible. I also, finally, understood that even though I never wanted to be a model, I had internalized this message to mean that I had limitations. The message made me think that achieving my career aspirations was going to be difficult because of my physical appearance.

Understanding the depth of how my inner critics impacted my beliefs *and* actions made way for not only seeing the truth, but for truly integrating it in my bones.

While this work goes deep and can benefit from a trusted guide holding space for you to do your discovery, here are a few steps you can take today, to learn more about your inner critics.

1. **Journal**: Write down all the things you say to yourself that bring you down, keep you feeling small, or make you feel anything other than pleased with yourself. Make note of the context – what you were doing, where you were, and who you were around. Do this for two weeks because, let me tell you, the exercise can be eye-opening when you see how you speak to yourself written on paper. Noting the contexts can help you pinpoint where you can expect to be triggered, which will provide a stronger chance to identify your strategy and take care of yourself.

2. **Create a Caricature**: Bring a full-picture to view your inner critics and name them one by one. Get creative with this and even have some FUN with it. I highly recommend NOT naming them after someone close to you – even if they have a strong resemblance. This will deepen your understanding by making parallels with where you may have received some of these messages, or the origin for when this inner critic was formed or strengthened further. If this calls to you, check out the book *Taming Your Gremlin*, by Rick Carlson. [2]

3. **Notice How You Feel**: Practice paying attention to how you feel when these messages pop in. If it's difficult in the moment, take stock at the end of the day and reflect on the emotional journey you went on. Pay attention to where in the body you feel these things. This offers clues for deeper understanding. I know it might not be your common practice to pay attention and listen to your body – but it holds valuable information. For example, if you realize you are feeling tightness in your throat, this could indicate that there is some work to do to feel comfortable in expressing yourself in certain situations. Perhaps there is also something to discover about when you may have been silenced or shut down in the past, which can be an indication that something needs healing from that experience.

Tara Mohr's book, *Playing Big* is a great resource and was an entry point for me in my own journey of better understanding my inner critics.[3]

Step 2: Internalize This Truth: You Are Not Your Inner Critic Voice

Clearly, this is easier said than done – I didn't say this was going to happen overnight – and it's a very important part of the journey. I'll share with you an experience that helped me with this internalization.

> *Before I had become an entrepreneur, and while I was working in Corporate, I had been looking hard at my life*

to understand what my next career move was going to be. I was considering the option of leaving my job to find out what else was possible.

I had a few coaches at that time to help me work through some of my blocks to quitting – because I KNEW I needed support on that journey. Right as I was nearing my self-imposed deadline to quit, my coach asked me for all the reasons why I was opposed to quitting. I blabbered on and on with all my reasons (ugly tears included). When I finished, I literally sat back in my chair, exhaled deeply and said "I don't believe ANY of that!" All the reasons I gave were all the messages my inner critic was telling me. And that was when I knew – I was not the same as my inner critic voices. My truth was somewhere buried underneath all of it.

Here are my top three tips to help you in separating yourself from your inner critic voices – to help you more concretely realize YOU are not those voices.

1. Add the words "My inner critic thinks that..." when your mind starts feeding you all the lies. This helps you remember that your true self is so much more than the part of you that is beating yourself up. The key is to do this frequently – as often as you notice those messages that aren't serving you.
2. When those terrible messages come through, DISRUPT the thought! STOP it as quickly as you can and by any means necessary. Remove it from your orbit. What do

I mean by that? I mean delete the damn thing in your mind! Send the thought right into the garbage can. Get out of your chair if you need to and physically move, as a way to honor and remember that you are not that thought, and that thought isn't true – it's a lie.

3. Look for the humor in the message. Find the ridiculousness and the absurdity. I know this might sound like a strange suggestion – but part of this work is to find the levity and to see things from a new perspective. It's one of those things where you can either cry or laugh about it – and I'm saying choose the latter. You see, inner critics often say things in absolutes and even make predictions they have no business making. This can sound something like "You will NEVER be able to..." Can you find the humor in someone being so matter-of-fact with you? Like, WTF do THEY know?

So, now you have started the work to truly know you are not your inner critic voice – that's awesome! For me, this was such a freeing discovery and it ignited my curiosity to know myself more intimately. Now it's time to fill your mind with the thoughts that actually serve you.

Step 3: Choose a New Message

This is the FUN part – the expansive part! Now you get to choose what you're going to start telling yourself INSTEAD of the inner critic messages that are holding you back. Call it a mantra, call it an affirmation, or simply call it a new thought. Whatever you call it, what you're doing is creating new tributaries in your mind, so you can create rivers of thoughts that actually serve you. You see, right now you got the Nile River running through your head, with the same old thoughts that have been flowing down it for years. There is an often referred to 2005 study from the National Science Foundation, which states; 95% of the thoughts we have were the same thoughts as the day before and of the approximate 60,000 thoughts we have in a day, 80% are negative.

What I need you to do is create new tributaries to create new rivers, so that your Nile River of lies starts drying the heck out. My suggestion around this is to choose something you can start to believe, as opposed to something you roll your eyes at. For example, let's say you are working on the inner critic that makes you feel like you can't reach a certain salary. You may want to consider a mantra like "I'm moving closer to my salary goals every day" versus something like "I am a billionaire" – which could at this moment feel very unattainable to you. Here's an example of what I mean.

> At one point during the pandemic, I told myself I wanted to be a global speaker (you see how that theme is reoccurring?). I decided to repeat this message to myself: "I am a global speaker." Not because I necessarily was, but because I could resonate with that vision. Not only did I say that to myself every time my inner critic was butting in, but I also took actions around that affirmation solidifying my intent. I purchased a whole

lighting system for my office because I could imagine speaking for a global audience, virtually. About six months later, I realized that dream did become a reality because I gave a workshop to hundreds of people with Creative Mornings™ – the world's largest face-to-face creative community, and there was most certainly a global audience present!

To reiterate, pick a new message that you want to claim for yourself. The bonus tip is to also take inspired and aligned action for those new rivers you are creating. Bring to life the new messages you are saying to yourself with physical reminders and micro steps towards the dreams you are bringing into reality.

These tips can support you in creating a better relationship with yourself! The one caveat I will give you is that transformation can be more potent and even more effective when you have a guide to help you through it. Impact comes when the exercises move from the mental conversations with yourself, to the physical embodiment of you, without your inner critics running the show. This is where working with a specialist such as a coach, therapist or somatic practitioner, can serve you in the unlock you seek.

So, how does all of this contribute to shifting workplace culture? Let's start with leadership. Based on a 2022 survey of over 13,000 employees, conducted by McKinsey, having an uncaring/uninspiring leader was in the top three reasons why they quit their previous job.[4]

How Inner Critic Work Supports Better Leadership

Inner critic work will help you to heal things from your past so you aren't bringing those things to the present day and sabotaging the now – let alone the future. It will bring levity to your life, and a deeper understanding of what needs to be unlocked to release more of your potential.

Doing inner critic work will help you show up to your workplace with more clarity of who you are and what you actually believe. It will allow your natural, authentic leadership style to come to the surface, so you can step more into who you are; versus who you think you're supposed to be.

Addressing inner critics' fears about relevance, stability and competence can pave the way to being less intimidated by others and uncertainty, and therefore more open to teaching and mentoring. The result of all of this is showing up more centered, grounded, and emotionally available for those that you lead.

Perhaps one of my clients put it best:

> "My work with Tosca began with self-confidence and being a more authentic person / leader. This evolved into unresolved history, inner critic work, limiting beliefs, setting boundaries, and bigger picture thinking. I have a new sense of self awareness, belief, and

acceptance. Moreover, bigger picture thinking has really helped me see all aspects of life differently, and more diversely. The most important element is the new level of peace, calm, and personal joy I have now. My leadership and management skills have evolved, resulting in an easier flow, and higher performance from myself and team. The saying 'Change yourself, change your world,' speaks to my life and the power of personal transformation."

Now let's talk about how your organization benefits from inner critic work, and how this new version of you has the potential to shift culture in a significant way.

Benefits of Inner Critic Work in Your Organization

When your inner critics show up less, you are single-handedly able to shift your environment because you are showing up differently. When your team(s) also receive training on inner critics – the impact becomes even greater. Here's a glimpse of that impact:

1. **Increased Confidence**: When employees see how they are holding themselves back and acknowledge the truth of their abilities, their natural confidence shines through. This leads to speaking up more, contributing ideas, and taking more proactive actions.

2. **Redefined Success**: When employees become more aware of their true needs and desires, they can redefine success for themselves. This often opens minds for non-linear opportunities, and fosters more awareness of the type of growth they need and desire. This can counter conditioned ideas such as upward mobility being the only indicator of success.

3. **Openness to Change**: Addressing deeply embedded fears helps pave the way to being open to new possibilities. If employees see alligators staring them in the face, it's going to be pretty hard for them to notice the oasis in the background that you are trying to draw their attention to.

4. **Greater Empathy**: This work lends itself to having more compassion and self-acceptance, and that leads to having more empathy for others. This can create a softening and a disarming, which leads employees to engage with their work and with others in a deeper, more meaningful way.

5. **Improved Relationships**: As employees have a better relationship with themselves, their relationships with others will inevitably improve over time. This is pretty much a guaranteed result of the work.

6. **Common Language**: When your workforce learns about inner critics and topics relating to it, they have common language to operate from to foster more vulnerable conversations about what might be happening below the surface. There is incredible power in being able to name the dynamics at play.

The benefits go well beyond this list. I am curious – what else can you see as the possible benefits with your own leadership, as well as your organization?

The Truth About Inner Critic Work

I've come to realize that while most people will raise their hands and say "I have inner critics!" – there are far fewer willing to do something meaningful about it. Here are some of the biggest barriers:

1. They think things can't change
2. They're worried they will be judged, and fearful about what they will discover about themselves
3. They don't know how to assess the return on their investment (of time and money)

As leaders, it's our responsibility to hold the space for the possibility that people can change, and that includes ourselves. Here's an extraordinary example of that.

> One of my clients – let's call her Sarah – was acutely aware that her predecessor was a toxic leader. A leader who led by fear, which resulted in employee behaviors that didn't actually serve the organization. While she was a heart-centered leader, Sarah embarked upon a coaching journey because she wanted to access greater confidence on the inside – even though she showcased

confidence externally. Over the course of six months, she had transformed so much that she experienced happiness at a level she never knew was possible. Not only that, but Sarah's team was no longer operating out of fear. They trusted her as well as their own capabilities. Sarah shifted the culture, single handedly.

Even with all this progress, in one session we stumbled upon deep seeded sadness – feelings that she had habitually avoided – fearful that it would drag her down into the abyss for good. She was extremely brave and decided to face it fully! The result? She unlocked a whole new level of inner confidence and acceptance of the complete career shift she had been dreaming of, yet had previously been too afraid to pursue.

Within my chapter, I have shared a lot of stories with you, but now I want to provide some questions to consider as you take stock of how all of this has landed within you. I encourage you to think about these, or better yet journal or even talk to a colleague about it.

- What has stuck with you from all that was shared?
- What resistance comes up when you consider going deeper with inner critic work?
- What next step(s) do you want to commit to as a courageous leader, related to inner critic work?
- Who in your life are you seeing differently, or who has come to mind?

The good news is your inner critic work has already started. Trust that what you have begun to reflect on in your own journey is exactly where you were meant to start. You're well on your way to shifting your relationship with your inner critics and becoming an even better leader – to yourself and to others. The waves of change in your business are a heartbeat away.

In Summary:

Inner critic work unlocks potential in leaders by:

- Revealing where they may be holding themselves back
- Unlocking their authentic confidence
- Increasing their willingness to speak up and take risks

Inner critic work shifts organizational culture by:

- Addressing the fears that inhibits openness to change
- Improving relationships
- Strengthening the empathetic leadership skill set

Recommended next steps:

- Reflect on what you learned from this chapter
- Share this chapter with colleagues and engage in conversations to discover threads of what might be playing out in your organization

- Determine what immediate next step would best serve you (ie. reading a book about this, engaging a coach, attending a workshop)

Notes

1. Lerner, Jennier S, et al. "Emotion and Decision Making | Annual Review of Psychology." Annual Review, 22 Sept. 2014, www.annualreviews.org/doi/10.1146/annurev-psych-010213-115043.
2. Carson, Rick. *Taming Your Gremlin.* Harper Collins, 2003.
3. Mohr, Tara. Playing Big. Random House UK, 2014.
4. https://www.mckinsey.com/capabilities/people-and-organizational-performance/our-insights/the-great-attrition-is-making-hiring-harder-are-you-searching-the-right-talent-pools

Dear Irma,

Thank you for all of your support through the years.

Your tenacity, generosity, capacity to learn and passion for life are all reasons why you inspire- not just me, but everyone you come in contact with.

As you enter a new chapter in your life, remember you are "MAGICAL AF and all things are possible. So send any inner critics that tell you otherwise on vacation.

SHINE ON, MY FRIEND!

Stay Feisty & fabulous,

Rosa J. Matteo

Tosca DiMatteo

Tosca DiMatteo is a transformational leadership and career coach, a speaker, and the founder of TOSCA Coaching and Consulting LLC. She has the trained mind of a brand marketer and is a keynote speaker who makes her audiences feel inspired to take new actions. She provides real actionable tips for how to do just that. She's a thought leader, an author, and a facilitator on the topics of personal and organizational transformation. Some of her most popular specialties include changing our relationship with our inner critics, holding boundaries, leading authentically, and brand building.

Tosca helps audiences feel empowered, confident, and more at ease traversing new growth trajectories. She has worked as a brand marketing executive for Fortune 500 companies such as Unilever, Kimberly Clark, Univision, Pernod Ricard (Absolut Vodka) and Wegmans Food Markets.

Tosca knows how personal transformation leads to career and business breakthroughs. Her track record includes leading diverse, cross-functional teams and renovating beloved global brands in highly competitive categories, as well as work with small businesses and personal brands across a variety of industries.

Tosca is ICF certified. She lives with her husband and dog in Brooklyn, New York.

Connect with Tosca DiMatteo:

LinkedIn: https://www.linkedin.com/in/toscadimatteo/

Website: https://toscadimatteo.com/

Newsletter Sign-Up: https://toscadimatteo.com/optin/

Blog: https://toscadimatteo.com/blog/

Instagram: https://www.instagram.com/toscadimatteo/

Email: breakthrough@toscadimatteo.com

7.

Impact Through Inclusion

Melanie Rodriguez, PhD | Talent Management, Leadership Coach, Inclusion Advocate

In today's increasingly diverse and interconnected world, inclusive leadership has become a critical component of creating a positive and effective organizational culture. Inclusive leadership is an approach that emphasizes the value of diversity, equity, and inclusion in the workplace and strives to create an environment where every employee feels valued, respected, and supported.

The growing recognition of the business case for diversity, equity, and inclusion highlights the critical nature of inclusive leadership. Research has shown that organizations with diverse and inclusive cultures are more innovative, have better financial performance, and are better equipped to meet the needs of their customers.[1] Furthermore, employees in inclusive workplaces report higher levels of job satisfaction, engagement, and commitment to their organization[2]. However, the impacts of an inclusive workplace extend far beyond what this research has measured. This can be seen in the societal expectations of corporate responses to the social justice environment events such as George Floyd, voting rights, and the overturning of Roe vs Wade. The truth is employees want to work for companies that share their values and who are not afraid to advocate for those values.

However, inclusive leadership is not something that has been historically taught in leadership programs. As a result, many leaders lack the necessary skills or understanding of how to promote diversity, equity, and inclusion and may inadvertently perpetuate biases or exclude certain groups. This is why many organizations are investing in DEI training programs to educate employees and create a more inclusive workplace. These trainings often focus on raising awareness of diversity and inclusion issues and providing employees with the tools to recognize and address biases. They have the potential to help an organization uncover hidden biases and address unfair hiring and development practices. They can also benefit company culture, boost growth potential, and support marginalized employees in their sense of belonging.

DEI training is a necessary step toward building an inclusive culture, but it also has limitations. The awareness of diversity and inclusion issues does not always translate into changes in behavior or the creation of an inclusive culture. The most successful organizational leaders go beyond DEI training to lead the way in fostering changes and holding the organization accountable for creating a more inclusive environment. They take the next step to integrate what they learn and become role models in the organization in order to create an organizational culture that people want to work for. This is what it means to be an Inclusive Leader.

Inclusive Leadership

Inclusive leadership is not just about hiring a diverse workforce, but about creating a culture where everyone can thrive. Leaders who exhibit inclusive behaviors and practices are better able to build and maintain diverse teams, encourage open communication, and promote a sense of belonging among all employees.

Inclusive leaders are individuals who demonstrate the ability to lead a diverse group of people with different backgrounds, beliefs, and values. They help build an organizational culture that brings diversity, equity, and inclusion to life. They prioritize creating an inclusive culture where every employee feels valued and respected.

Inclusive Leadership Principles

There are four main principles that show up in inclusive leadership. They are:

- Presence
- Courageous Leadership
- Championing Change
- A Systems Mindset

Presence is a term that, here, describes a leader's ability to be fully present at the moment; both physically and mentally. It involves being aware of one's own thoughts, feelings, and behaviors, as well as being attentive to the needs of others. Leaders who are present are more effective communicators, problem solvers, and decision-makers – as they are better able to connect with their team members and understand their perspectives.

Courageous leadership involves taking risks and making decisions that challenge the status quo, even if they are unpopular or uncomfortable. It requires leaders to be willing to speak up when they see injustice or discrimination and to advocate for marginalized groups who may not have a voice. It also involves being vulnerable and authentic, showing empathy and compassion for others, and creating a sense of psychological safety where people feel free to express their ideas and opinions.

Championing change involves creating a workplace environment that is responsive to changing conditions and values diverse perspectives and ideas. Leaders who champion change encourage their employees to think creatively, take risks, and challenge the status quo. They also provide the necessary resources, tools, and support to help their employees work effectively in a changing environment.

Having a Systems Mindset is the practical application of systems thinking, a framework that enables leaders to see the world as a complex and interconnected system. It involves understanding the relationships and interdependencies between different elements within the system and how they work together to produce certain outcomes. When applied to leadership, systems thinking can help leaders identify and address the root causes of inequality and exclusion, develop innovative solutions to complex problems, and promote a culture of inclusivity and collaboration.

How does that really materialize in a workplace? Take, for example, Andy, a client that is the CIO of a northeastern mid-sized tech company. Andy realized that his organization's inclusion efforts were not playing out as the company had hoped, despite their efforts in DEI training.

The training was a company reaction to low scores on the employee engagement survey. Based on the survey outcomes, the business contracted with a well-known company that provides DEI training. The senior leadership team and next-level managers were required to attend this training within the first six months of the company working with the DEI training entity. Andy was part of this cohort of leaders that went through the training.

As a result, Andy learned about what inclusion meant for

the company and committed to supporting inclusion efforts going forward. He became the sponsor for an employee resource group and was even quoted in the company newsletter discussing the importance of inclusion. However, as CIO, Andy's calendar and workload was often over-committed and he was over-extended. As the year progressed, the DEI efforts Andy committed to slipped lower and lower on the list of priorities. While Andy knew they were important, the truth was that those things he committed to were considered "extracurricular" on his performance assessment. With the big shift in the company's IT Service Delivery Model coming up, he felt the pressure to make sure everything went smoothly.

One day, Andy received a message from someone in his business unit. An employee who was part of the employee network he sponsored was looking for support on an initiative they wanted to pursue. The email ended with "I realize this is a low priority for you, but it would really help these employees feel seen." Andy saw that line and paused. It was that brief line that made Andy stop and reflect on his DEI journey. He recognized that simply checking off boxes and taking mandatory training was not enough to create real change within the organization. He knew he needed to do a better job of leading by example and integrating inclusive behaviors into his daily leadership practices.

Andy took it upon himself to find a coach – someone to help him work through what it meant for him to be an inclusive leader. Together, they worked on the four principles of inclusive leadership and found ways to make them real and doable for who he is as a leader.

Presence

Presence is a critical component of inclusive leadership as it allows leaders to build stronger relationships with team members, foster innovation, and nurture an environment where team members feel valued and respected. By being present and paying attention, leaders are better able to manage diverse teams because they are able to adapt their leadership style to meet the needs of different team members. This takes some time and effort. It takes leaders being intentional about how they reflect on their own leadership style and creating awareness around how they "show up."

The first step in understanding your presence as a leader is self-awareness. It involves being aware of one's own thoughts, feelings, and behaviors, as well as being attentive to the needs of others. Leaders who are self-aware are better able to understand their own biases and assumptions; which enables them to build more authentic relationships with team members. This awareness comes from being open to being vulnerable, listening to feedback, and leveraging assessments to learn about yourself in new ways.

Authenticity is another important competency for developing a presence in inclusive leadership. Leaders who are authentic are able to be themselves, and they encourage others to do the same and be boldly, and authentically **them**. Authentic leaders are honest, transparent, and trustworthy; this helps to build strong relationships with team members.

Leaders with a strong presence demonstrate confidence in all that they do. They are able to make decisions quickly and effectively, which helps to build momentum and drive innovation. Leaders who are confident inspire trust and respect from team members.

Leaders with a presence are also often seen as charismatic. Charismatic leaders are able to inspire and motivate team members, which helps to build a positive and engaged work environment. They are able to communicate a clear vision and bring others along on the journey.

Adaptability is also essential for developing a presence in inclusive leadership. Leaders who are adaptable are able to adjust their leadership style to meet the needs of different team members. They are able to be flexible and responsive to changing circumstances. This helps to build trust and respect from team members.

Courageous Leadership

Courageous leadership is important for creating an inclusive workplace culture in that it helps to break down barriers and create a sense of belonging for **everyone**. When leaders are willing to take risks and challenge the status quo, they can create an environment where everyone feels valued, respected, and supported. This can increase employee engagement, foster innovation, and creativity, as well as improve overall organizational performance.

In addition, courageous leadership can help to address the persistent problem of workplace discrimination and bias. When leaders are willing to speak up and advocate for marginalized groups, they can help to create a more equitable and just workplace culture. This can help to improve employee retention, attract new talent, and enhance the organization's reputation in the marketplace.

So, what practical steps can people take in their work to integrate inclusive practices and become more courageous leaders, and practice being an upstander?

- Start by educating yourself about the experiences of marginalized groups in the workplace. This can involve reading articles, attending training sessions or workshops, or engaging in conversations with people from different backgrounds. By understanding the perspectives of others, you can become more empathetic and informed, and be better equipped to advocate for inclusive practices.

- If you witness discrimination or microaggressions in the workplace, speak up and address the issue. This can involve having a difficult conversation with a colleague or manager or raising concerns with HR or a diversity and inclusion committee. By taking action, you can help to create a culture where everyone feels safe and valued.
- Look for opportunities to challenge the status quo and create a more inclusive workplace culture. This could involve advocating for diversity and inclusion in hiring and promotion decisions, creating employee resource groups or affinity networks, or implementing policies and practices that promote equity and justice.
- Finally, it is important to hold yourself and others accountable for creating an inclusive workplace culture. This can involve setting measurable goals and tracking progress, conducting regular assessments of workplace diversity and inclusion, and addressing any issues or challenges that arise.

Championing Change

Championing change is a critical component of inclusive leadership, as it enables leaders to create a culture that fosters continuous improvement, encourages open communication, and supports the development of diverse and innovative teams.

Leaders can foster a culture of innovation by encouraging their employees to be creative, take risks, and share their ideas. They can provide training and resources to support creativity and innovation, recognize and reward innovative ideas, and create a safe space for experimentation.

Leaders can encourage open communication by providing regular opportunities for employees to share their ideas, concerns, and feedback. Leaders can listen actively, be receptive to feedback, and provide constructive responses.

Leaders can emulate championing change by modeling the behaviors they want to see in their employees. They can be transparent and authentic in their communication, demonstrate a willingness to learn and adapt, and take action to address any issues or concerns that arise.

With the increasing prevalence of remote work and digital transformation, leaders can champion change by embracing technology and adapting to new ways of working. They can provide the necessary resources, tools, and support to help their employees work effectively from home or other remote locations. They can also encourage the use of digital technologies to promote collaboration, communication, and innovation.

Systems Thinking

To promote a culture of inclusivity, leaders must move beyond traditional problem-solving methods and adopt a holistic approach to understanding the complex and interdependent systems within their organization. This is where systems thinking comes into play.

One of the main reasons why systems thinking is essential in inclusive leadership is because it helps leaders identify and address the root causes of inequality and exclusion. Traditional problem-solving methods often focus on treating symptoms rather than addressing the underlying causes of problems. However, when leaders use a systems thinking approach, they can analyze the complex relationships between different elements within the organization and its larger context to identify the root causes of problems. For example, instead of simply addressing a lack of diversity in the workplace, a leader using systems thinking might examine the recruitment and hiring process, cultural norms and values, and systemic barriers that might be preventing a diverse workforce from being hired and/or retained. By addressing the root causes of problems, leaders can develop more sustainable and effective solutions that promote inclusivity and equity.

In addition, systems thinking can also help leaders develop innovative solutions to complex problems. In today's business environment, leaders are faced with a wide range of complex and multifaceted problems that cannot be solved through traditional problem-solving methods. By using a systems thinking approach, leaders can identify opportunities for collaboration and innovation across different departments and teams. They can encourage cross-functional teams to work together to develop solutions that take into account the interdependencies between different elements within the organization and its larger context. This can lead to more innovative and effective solutions that promote inclusivity, equity, and sustainability.

Furthermore, systems thinking can help leaders promote a culture of inclusivity and collaboration within the organization. By using a systems thinking approach, leaders can encourage collaboration and teamwork across different departments and teams. They can foster a culture of open communication and active listening, which can help build trust and promote a sense of ownership and commitment to the organization's goals. By promoting a culture of inclusivity and collaboration, leaders can help to create an environment where employees feel empowered to contribute their unique perspectives and ideas.

To integrate inclusive practices into their work, leaders can take practical steps to develop a systems-thinking mindset. Leaders can develop a comprehensive understanding of the organization by examining the interdependence of different elements within the organization. Such as policies, procedures, and practices. They can use data and feedback to identify patterns and trends and understand how different elements within the organization are interconnected.

Leaders can identify and address the root causes of problems by analyzing the complex relationships between different elements within the organization and its larger context. This can involve examining the cultural norms and values within the organization, as well as identifying systemic barriers that might be preventing inclusivity and equity.

Leaders can use a holistic approach to problem-solving by examining the organization as a whole rather than focusing on isolated problems or individual departments. This can help leaders identify opportunities for collaboration and innovation across different departments and teams.

Leaders can also encourage collaboration and cross-functional teams to promote systems thinking and develop innovative solutions to complex problems. This can involve creating opportunities for employees to work together on projects and initiatives, as well as providing training and support to develop the necessary skills and mindsets for systems thinking.

Andy's Story

To close, let's circle back to Andy and his experience with DEI and his efforts to become an inclusive leader. One of the key changes that Andy implemented was creating a diversity, equity, and inclusion task force within the company. The task force was made up of employees from different departments and levels of the organization, and their goal was to identify areas where the company could improve in terms of diversity, equity, and inclusion. Andy made it clear that the task force had his full support and that their recommendations would be taken seriously. This time Andy made sure that this was more than just lip service.

Andy knew that integrating the recommendations from the task force would take more than a town hall speech and an email. It would take making sure that inclusive behaviors were recognized and rewarded. It also meant that there needed to be something measurable that people could point to when having performance conversations at the end of the year.

By integrating inclusive leadership principles, Andy was able to create an impact that was not only seen within the organization but also in the company's bottom line. The company began to see a shift in its culture. Employees were more engaged and felt they had a voice in the organization. The company's internal reputation improved, and employee satisfaction was boosted tremendously.

Notes

1. Schwartz, Jeff, et al. "Returning to Work in the Future of Work." Deloitte Insights, 15 May 2020, www2.deloitte.com/us/en/insights/focus/human-capital-trends/2020/covid-19-and-the-future-of-work.html.

2. https://www.catalyst.org/reports/workplace-diversity-equity-inclusion-accountability-fair-processes/

Melanie Rodriguez

Melanie is a professionally certified, ICF coach who is passionate about empowering others to be the type of leader people want to work for. As an Organizational and Talent Development Specialist of over 19 years, Melanie serves as an executive coach and consultant in the areas of:

- inclusion,
- leadership development,
- systems change, and
- organizational capability.

Melanie's experience spans operations, commercial, IT, talent management, government, health care, and academia. She brings a wealth of knowledge about multicultural, multi-ethnic, and multi-generational differences. Melanie's knowledge encompasses how to leverage and integrate them to create organizational cultures that value the individual while also building a sense of belonging for all.

Melanie graduated from the University of Houston with a B.A. in Public Relations/Advertising and a minor in Mexican American Studies. She earned an M.A. in Organizational Management from the University of Phoenix, and an M.A. in Human Development, and a Ph.D. Human & Organizational Systems from Fielding Graduate University.

Connect with Melanie Rodriguez:

LinkedIn: https://www.linkedin.com/in/melanie-rodriguez-phd/

Email: melanie@elevatelatinas.com

8.

Culture Repair

The New Mandate

Rita Ernst | Positivity Influencer

My dad is an extraordinary handyman. For as long as I can remember, he has given his time and skills to helping neighbors and friends with their home repair and renovation projects. Got a leaking faucet? My dad can fix that. Have some deck boards rotting or coming loose? He can install a whole new deck for you. Need a drywall patch? Not his favorite task, but he can do a passable job. These are examples of the commonly accepted definition of repair: fixing or restoring something to working order.

Since 2020, workplaces and workforce-members' expectations have shifted dramatically. Necessity is the mother of invention, and remote working to prevent the spread of a deadly pathogen was the burning platform that catapulted us into a new work reality guided by these three vital changes:

1. With the elimination of external childcare resources, people learned to harmonize the competing commitments of work and family in new ways.
2. Grace for imperfection became a norm as pets, children, and passing spouses photo-bombed and, sometimes, interrupted work meetings.
3. Fluidity and flexibility replaced the traditional eight to ten hour days sitting in a company office pretending that nothing else exists of importance except your job.

This experience voided people's tolerance of traditional employment practices. You may be among those people voting with your feet against employers and cultures resisting flexibility and pursuing profits at any cost. Recent trends such as "the Great Resignation" and quiet quitting make this tectonic shift visible. People are rejecting the norm of workplace stress and setting boundaries around employers' demands on their time and attention. The result is workplaces with historically low levels of employee engagement, a measure of how connected, motivated, and committed you are to give your time and talent to your workplace. The 2022 employee engagement results measured by the Gallup organization reported these troubling trends:

> *"The ratio of engaged to actively disengaged workers in the U.S. is 1.8-to-1, down from 2.1-to-1 in 2021 and 2.6-to-1 in 2020. This is the lowest ratio of engaged to actively disengaged employees in the U.S. since 2013, almost a decade earlier."* [1]

So, my use of the word *repair* might make you think this chapter is about getting back to how things used to be. Not exactly. Contemplate this alternative definition of the word repair using the Latin root, *reparāre*. 'Re' means to do again, and '*parāre*' means to make ready. When you put it together, you get a completely different definition – to make ready again. This is what I mean when I say *"Culture repair is the new mandate"* because culture is not set in stone. It isn't work you do once, dust off your hands, and leave on autopilot. Culture is dynamic and ever-evolving, and your organization must be prepared to adapt synchronously.

The historical practices of mandating culture through policies and proclamations represent defunct mental models that treat culture as a problem that needs to be fixed. Conformity isn't the path to organizational well-being. Nor are today's workers willing to comply with edicts that contradict their individual values. **Think about it. You don't want to be told how you must act; you want your best self to be inspired to show up at work.**

So, if your job as a leader isn't to fix the culture but to prepare it again, what's the assignment? I am so glad you asked!

Culture repair is creating the context for a positive environment where your business thrives because your team members:

- achieve and put forth their full potential
- support and inspire one another to contribute fully
- experience individual and collective well-being*

(*91% of respondents to Indeed's Workplace Happiness Survey said how they feel at work impacts how they feel at home.) [2]

Notice your job isn't to do or to dictate. Rather, you set the conditions and are a catalyst to activate your team.

In *Show Up Positive*, my first book on culture and the power of individuals to create the workplace they desire through the cultivation of positive thoughts and actions, I assert that every team member is an architect of the culture:

> *"You are the culture, and the culture is you. It reflects the assumptions, beliefs, and behaviors of the people who make up the organization – and that's you!"* [3] *[pp. 24]*

Congratulations! This is wonderful news because you now have a ready-made group of collaborators. You are released from the job of telling and selling, focusing instead on activating and co-creating.

There are three essential elements to a positive, healthy, and vibrant organizational culture:

1. Belongingness – the extent to which individuals have a community that fully accepts and welcomes them

2. Contribution – being appreciated and invited to share your gifts and talents fully
3. Alliance – feeling ownership for and commitment to the organization

Let's examine each of these more closely.

Belongingness

Belongingness occurs when people experience the security in knowing they are accepted and supported as a group member. **In Abraham Maslow's need hierarchy theory, belongingness is your third-level need, preceded only by your food, shelter, and safety requirements.**

Self
Actualization

Esteem Needs

Belonging Needs

Safety Needs

Physiological Needs

Yet, an alarming 40% of respondents who completed the 2019 Ernst & Young Belonging Barometer Study reported physical and emotional isolation at work.[4]

At the 2023 World Happiness Summit, Sarah Cunningham, the managing director of the World Well-being Movement, cited belonging as the number one driver of well-being at work. This assertion is consistent with the following employee engagement data from the Gallup Organization:

Having a best friend at work significantly correlates with:

- likelihood to recommend their workplace
- probability of staying with the company
- overall satisfaction with their workplace[5]

In case that isn't enough to convince you of the value of cultivating belonging in your workplace, consider these statistics from research conducted by BetterUp, which correlates belonging with:

- a 56% increase in job performance
- a 50% reduction in turnover risk
- a 75% decrease in employee sick days[6]

Contribution

Contribution is easily determined by your answer to the question, "Do you consider the work you do important?" The 2021 Workplace Happiness Study, commissioned by Indeed and conducted by Forrester Consulting, found that **feeling energized by your work and having a sense of purpose were the top-ranking factors contributing to people's happiness at work**.[7] Consider these burnout statistics from research conducted by SurveyMonkey. 94% of employees who found their work meaningful didn't experience burnout, while 75% of those who lacked meaningfulness at work did.[8] It is essential to understand that an individual's connection to the purpose of what they are doing – beyond simply completing tasks – determines meaningfulness, not the content of their work.

Another important fact is the correlation between your happiness and well-being. In *Happier Hour* , Dr. Cassie Holmes shares what her research uncovered as she sought to determine whether escaping to a quiet life on the beach would make her happier.[9] Surprisingly, she and her fellow researchers discovered that having too much discretionary time generates as much unhappiness as being time-starved.

> *"In a follow-up experiment that Hal, Marissa, and I conducted, we found that lacking a sense of productivity is why people with excessive amounts of available time feel less satisfied in their lives. Regularly having more*

than 5 hours of discretionary time in a day is too much because it undermines one's sense of purpose." [pp. 8-9]

Recognition, a form of external validation, reinforces purposefulness at work. In a 2016 study by OGO, 82% of respondents felt under-recognized at work. However, 40% said they would put more energy into their job if their recognition increased.[10] There is much more on the line here than an increase in work effort. The 2021 Engagement and Retention Report by Achievers includes the staggering finding that lack of recognition is the number one reason 69% of respondents plan to switch jobs. This is the perfect segue to the final essential element of a positive, healthy, and vibrant organizational culture.

Alliance

Alliance is about allegiance – a person's desire and commitment to continue being a part of your team and company. It matters because losing a team member hits the bottom line in multiple ways. In 2021 Gallup gave employers the guiding expense of 1.5 to 2 times a worker's salary to replace them.[11] However, this is only part of the economic story. That number fails to include other costs, including:

- lowered morale
- increased stress on remaining staff
- delays resulting from insufficient staff

- mistakes resulting from insufficiently trained staff
- decreased customer happiness due to reduced experience
- decreased operational efficiencies and effectiveness

In 2019 LinkedIn analyzed 32 million profiles to determine the primary contributors to retention (a.k.a organizational alliance). Here's what they found.[12]

- Internal movement (even laterally) significantly increases retention for up to five years.
- Managers with high ratings for openness and effectiveness develop greater staff alliance.
- Companies that prioritize workplace autonomy get longer employee tenure.

Many factors affect alliance. Notice in the Cultural Harmony image below the interconnectedness of belongingness, contribution, and alliance. Rather than existing discreetly, they influence and are influenced by one another. The consistent color indicates alignment, and the darker coloring at their points of intersection depicts their bonded strength.

In contrast, the Cultural Dis-harmony image below illustrates the weakening bonds that occur when an element (in this instance, contribution) is at risk or unfulfilled. As contribution declines, alliance with the organization as a whole quickly follows the same trajectory. As we learned above, a decline in belongingness would affect alliance similarly.

Cultural Harmony

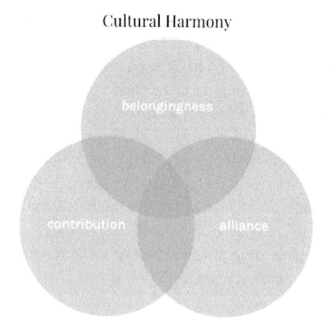

Cultural Dis-harmony

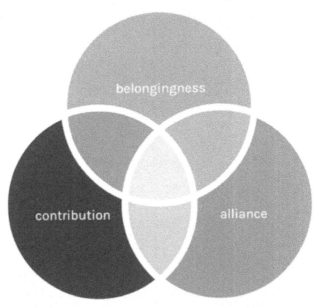

The Culture Repair Model

Are you beginning to grasp and understand the compelling case for leadership attention to cultivating workplace cultures that foster belongingness, contribution, and alliance? Undoubtedly, avoiding the burdensome costs of turnover and disengagement is best. To help you, I developed the culture repair model, illustrated below, which focuses on these three essential drivers of workplace happiness and well-being. This model details the reinforcers to increase each element and the KPIs that act as a warning system that one or more of these elements is in decline.

Let me walk you through it.

Your team's belongingness, contribution, and alliance are not fixed. Just as these can grow, they also can diminish. Erosion coincides with the disruption of people's positive thoughts and behaviors. They form new assumptions, conclusions, and beliefs as they work to make sense of their experience. These change the stories teammates tell about the team and workplace, emphasizing their dismay and discontent.

Even what you perceive as a minor incident can become a disrupting event that sets your culture on the death march.

The reason is that individual responses to change vary greatly. What seems inconsequential to you can be earth-shattering to your team member. Here's a simple personal example from my recent trip to Italy.

Home Away from Home

This year, I attended the World Happiness Summit held in Lake Como, Italy. After spending the start of the trip with a colleague for sightseeing and the conference, on the evening of day seven, I found myself alone in Milan. I had two more days before catching my return flight home, and admittedly, I felt a little lonely and guilty for extending my stay.

It was happy hour in Italy, so I used Google search to find a restaurant within close walking distance of my new hotel. Just around the corner, I entered Re Fosco Bistrot and ordered a glass of Prosecco. As I sipped my wine, I planned my itinerary for the next two days.

It was a Sunday, and the restaurant was mildly busy. It was cozy with a quiet ambiance that could have made me feel conspicuous as the only solo patron and tourist, but it didn't. I soon flagged the waiter to request another. A second server arrived with an open bottle and refilled my glass. I immediately had the nostalgia of being with friends and decided to stay for dinner.

The next time the waiter passed, I asked for a dinner menu. My eggplant parmesan arrived with a smile and a glass of water. I savored the food and atmosphere and decided to return the following evening. As I settled the bill, I praised the food and service and answered a few polite questions about myself. I was walking out the door when I declared, "See you tomorrow."

Re Fosco Bistrot was buzzing the following evening with tables of friends gathered for after-work drinks. I smiled and warmly greeted my two servers, "I'm back!" They returned my smile and gave attention to finding the perfect spot for me to sit.

This time as my glass of Prosecco arrived, I also received the aperitivo menu. I had seen these handwritten menus on other tables the prior evening. The waiter translated the chef's special three-tasting menu. I suddenly felt like a local, imagining this as my place to hang out regularly.

Alone and a continent away from my family, I experienced belonging. And for me, the most beautiful part is that we were all just being ourselves. I discovered an inviting warmth in the service that was enticing. Refilling my glass at my table was standard practice for them, but it signified much more to me. Rather than dismissing me as a passing tourist, they reciprocated my openness and won my loyalty.

On my final night, I arrived at Re Fosco Bistrot and didn't see either of the servers from my previous visits. I ordered my Prosecco and scrolled through my phone, *feeling slightly disappointed. Once again, I was just a tourist and had to inquire about the aperitivo menu. My prior evening's bliss of belonging was rapidly deflating.*

As I sipped my wine and awaited my food, I spied my Prosecco steward walking through the restaurant. He looked in my direction, and I smiled and waved. He returned my smile and was soon at my table with the Prosecco bottle in hand and my belonging restored. It was that simple—just one person who knew me and whose treatment signaled to others that I was no longer an outsider.

Unlike the story I just shared, you can't depend on faltering belongingness, contribution and alliance experiences to right themselves. Monitoring for decline is crucial to making swift course corrections that restore business results and personal and organizational well-being. Here's a brief introduction to the performance indicators of the death march, located in the bottom half of the chart. These include observable behaviors as well as traditional business performance measures.

When team members lose their belongingness, you see:

- Absenteeism on the rise
- Scorekeeping – keeping track of co-workers' attitudes and behaviors to justify disgruntlement and call out disparities in work ethic
- Low morale – visible in complaints, poor attitudes, and

decreased energy within the team

When team members withdraw their contributions, you see:

- Quality issues such as mistakes increasing
- Missed deadlines
- Angry and disappointed customers

When team members question their desire for alliance, you see:

- Turnover at a higher rate, including the loss of your best people
- Toxic behaviors such as coalition building and rumor-mongering
- Lost business opportunities due to team inefficiencies and low performance

Traditional management practices teach you to respond to decreased quality, productivity, and growth with system and process changes. Asking yourself, "Can we do this with fewer steps, automate, or reduce redundancies?" has value but is insufficient because it ignores the number one contributor to success: your people.

Businesses must recognize and prioritize engaging their people more frequently in order to resolve performance decline. I'm not advocating for the typical actions such as rule-making and compliance. These are the wrong conversations to have resulting in the wrong solutions.

There is a better, faster, and more sustainable approach: conversations to increase connection and commitment. Here is a recent client story to bring this to life.

Merger or Takeover?

The shared directive was to merge two complimentary yet distinct operations into one facility. The selected site was newer and had excess capacity. Looking at the P&L, the economies of scale and efficiencies gained were undeniable. Additionally, each team had a stellar track record of service and teamwork.

No one could deny the logic, yet the teams from each facility were full of anxiety and fear. Early conversations uncovered many operational differences. The team at the selected location was smaller than the team relocating, so they feared being outvoted. The relocating team worried about "home court advantage" diminishing their voice.

Although having management evaluate procedures and decide which to adopt would facilitate quicker decisions, these leaders understood that the resistance and dissatisfaction of their team members would cause many implementation issues. Additionally, differences in the work required adaptations to allow paperwork and practices that met the newly combined needs.

Here's the approach they used:

1. Managers prioritized the procedure and paperwork changes.
2. Managers formed a small review team that included team members with direct knowledge.
3. The review team identified all the needs and current procedures, then determined the new methods integrating the best from historical practices.
4. The broader team received communication about the new method, including an opportunity to understand why changes occurred.

> I facilitated a conversation early in this process when team members complained that the group dismissed the input of their representative. Being present at the meeting, the representative quickly corrected this misperception. She confirmed her full support for the new process and explained some of the changes her teammates challenged as invalid.
>
> The result was a significant reduction in the number of team members complaining and actively resisting this change. And when it was time to implement, the team's attention stayed focused on fixing the implementation issues rather than debating the decision's merits.

One additional guidance as you assess using the metrics listed in the culture repair model is to remember that indicators don't always direct you to discrete issues. Workplace satisfaction results from the interplay of all three elements (belongingness, contribution, and alliance). Use these KPIs as a starting place to engage with curiosity and learn what people are actually and genuinely experiencing. Remember, you are not on a fact-finding mission to figure out what is broken and fix it. Instead, focus on guiding your team to identify and manifest the workplace culture they want through their behaviors and shared experiences.

The **#ShowUpPositive** actions listed in the upper section of the culture repair model above are the drivers you can use as a leader to repair and reinforce belongingness, contribution, and alliance. Lead with these actions in response to one of the aforementioned decline measures. Even when things are going smoothly, make them a routine part of your daily and weekly interactions with your team.

To improve and sustain belongingness:

- Make expressing gratitude a consistent practice within the team.
- Establish open, two-way communication with a 2 to 1 listening-to-speaking ratio as the leader.
- Align your systems, processes, and rewards to make teamwork the priority.

To improve and sustain contribution:

- Be trustworthy, give trust freely, and create psychological safety for all.
- Give accountability and decision-making to those closest to the work (don't micro-manage).

- Vocalize your appreciation for the individual strengths and gifts of each team member and look for ways to leverage those more fully.

To improve and sustain alliance:

- Celebrate all the forward progress, not just the major milestones.
- Offer systems and processes to make recognition a daily norm practiced by all team members.
- Set team goals and rewards to express thanks for the team's efforts and carry the momentum forward.

Conclusion

Workers today have spoken – loudly. They are interested in something other than jobs and companies where they are simply a cog in the wheel. They want autonomy and ownership, pride and appreciation, and the satisfaction of knowing their work makes a difference. They want to feel seen, heard, understood, and valued for all they bring to their work.

Teams and organizations require people. Your team members are the essential ingredient for success. Workplace well-being happens when there is an even exchange of value between what people give and what they receive in return. Money is only a tiny component of that value equation. Instead, focus on what people want – happiness and fulfillment. Overall happiness and fulfillment comes from purpose, belonging, and the ability to do what brings them joy.

Although this sounds straightforward, many stumbling blocks along the path can derail workplace happiness. This makes it essential for teams and leaders to give specific attention to the conditions that create shared well-being and to cultivate those experiences intentionally and regularly. I call this work culture repair – to prepare again the context and environment that satisfies our human needs for belongingness, contribution, and alliance.

Whether your team is zooming ahead or struggling to right itself after a dip in performance, forget the old playbook and focus on the culture repair model instead. I guarantee you will see faster results and increase your organizational resilience to overcome future challenges when you and your team co-create a positive workplace where everyone:

- achieves and makes available their full potential
- supports and inspires one another to contribute fully
- experiences individual and collective well-being.

TL;DR

- We have entered a new era of work that requires a different value exchange between employers and workers.
- The old playbook and workplace norms are defunct, resulting in higher turnover, disengagement, and added costs.
- Workplace culture is not fixed because disrupting events can derail workplace happiness, making it essential for teams and leaders to give specific attention to the conditions that create shared well-being and to cultivate those experiences intentionally and regularly.
- The new mandate for managers and leaders is culture repair: creating the context for a positive environment where your business thrives because your team members:
  - achieve and put forth their full potential
  - support and inspire one another to contribute fully
  - experience individual and collective well-being
- Culture repair requires attentiveness to the three essential elements of positive, healthy, and vibrant organizational cultures:
  - belongingness – the extent to which individuals have a community that fully accepts and welcomes them
  - contribution – being appreciated and invited to

share your gifts and talents fully
  ◦ alliance – feeling ownership for and commitment to the organization
- In the Culture Repair Model, there are reinforcers to increase each element and the KPIs that act as a warning system that one or more of these elements is in decline.

Notes

1. Harter, Jim. "U.S. Employee Engagement Needs a Rebound in 2023." Gallup.Com, 9 May 2023, www.gallup.com/workplace/468233/employee-engagement-needs-rebound-2023.aspx.

2. Indeed Editorial Team. "The Great Realization: Is Happiness at Work Possible? - Indeed." Indeed, 19 Sept. 2022, ca.indeed.com/career-advice/career-development/work-happiness-survey.

3. ERNST, RITA. Show Up Positive. Ignite Your Extraordinary, 2022.

4. "The Surprising Power of Simply Asking Coworkers How They're Doing." Harvard Business Review, 21 Mar. 2019, hbr.org/2019/02/the-surprising-power-of-simply-asking-coworkers-how-theyre-doing.

5. Plowman, Stephanie, and Alok Patel. "The Increasing Importance of a Best Friend at Work." Gallup.Com, 20 Apr. 2023, www.gallup.com/workplace/397058/increasing-importance-best-friend-work.aspx.

6. Johnson, Whitney, et al. "The Value of Belonging at Work." Harvard Business Review, 21 Dec. 2021, hbr.org/2019/12/the-value-of-belonging-at-work.

7. Indeed Editorial Team. "The Great Realization: Is Happiness at Work Possible? - Indeed." Indeed, 19 Sept. 2022,

ca.indeed.com/career-advice/career-development/work-happiness-survey.

8. "5 Ways to Reduce Job Burnout among Your Employees." SurveyMonkey, www.surveymonkey.com/mp/reducing-employee-job-burnout/#:~:text=Give%20meaningful%20work%20assignments.,find%20their%20work%20meaningful%20have. Accessed 24 May 2023.

9. HOLMES, CASSIE. Happier Hour: How to Beat Distraction, Expand Your Time, and Focus on What Matters Most. GALLERY BOOKS, 2023.

10. "Ogo Recognition Deficit Survey Research Results - PWR New Media." O Great One, Mar. 2016, ogo.new-media-release.com/launch/downloads/OGO_Survey.pdf.

11. Robison, Vipula Gandhi and Jennifer. "The 'great Resignation' Is Really the 'Great Discontent.'" Gallup.Com, 6 Apr. 2023, www.gallup.com/workplace/351545/great-resignation-really-great-discontent.aspx.

12. "3 Factors Strongly Linked to Better Employee Retention, According to 32 Million LinkedIn Profiles." LinkedIn, 20 Nov. 2019, www.linkedin.com/business/talent/blog/talent-strategy/factors-linked-to-better-employee-retention.

Rita Ernst

Rita Ernst owns Ignite Your Extraordinary, an organizational consulting practice emphasizing the convergence of happiness and productivity to create positive, committed, high-performing organizations. She was named a Top Influential Leader of 2022 by TAP-In Magazine and Most Positive Management Consultancy of the Year 2023 – USA in Acquisition International's Influential Businesswoman Awards. Rita holds an advanced degree in Organizational Psychology from Clemson University and has been featured as an expert on Forbes and MSNBC. Her professional credits include adjunct professor for graduate and undergraduate classes, publication in national magazines, and featured podcast guest. Her first book, Show Up Positive, was released on June 14, 2022.

Connect with Rita Ernst:

LinkedIn: https://www.linkedin.com/in/rita-ernst-positivity-influencer/

Website: www.igniteextraordinary.com

9.

Team Impact

Bridging Culture "Full Team Ahead"

Susan LePlae Miller | Values Culture and Business Consultant, Author and Poet

Entrepreneurs and company leaders are facing the challenge of how best to maximize their impact while working across a multigenerational and multicultural workforce.

There are currently five generations actively employed, and the global footprint of employees and customers has extended with the use of technology. From email to video calls, and social media, speaking with employees and clients globally has become common and expected. Where does one begin to build a team that can evolve with these changing times? The stage has broadened from a regional to a hybrid-global model. Leaders are recognizing the importance of building cultural bridges in order to create and maintain a healthy culture that can thrive and succeed.

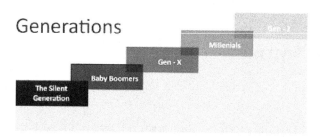

1

From the moment a candidate meets our company for the first time, either online or in-person, to the day they walk out the door, the way we treat them will be etched in their brain as the "Company Brand." In the marketing world, your brand is your identity and key differentiator. The revolution of technology is creating a fiercely competitive landscape of cost efficiencies combined with the desire to attract and retain the best and brightest. A happy workforce can produce higher performance, better efficiency, creative teamwork, and new ideas. An unhappy workforce can create a revolving door of talent and a myriad of unpleasant tasks and costs to accompany employee turnover.

How do we improve the employee experience to capitalize on our most valuable resources: people? Certainly, it is helpful to have an understanding of how the mission, vision, and values of the organization intersect with the mission, vision and values of the individual. Each company has a certain set of beliefs and purpose in mind for what problem they are solving for, how they plan to carry out the mission, who it is for, and why they are doing it.

Inherent in this process is a set of core values that are present to help evolve and differentiate the offering. Developing a deeper understanding of the core values helps in all facets of decision-making, from the voice of the company to other business and HR decisions. Values are an important consideration in the assembly of teammates and partners, both inside and outside the organization.

While seeking teammates, it is helpful to remember each person is unique and gifted with specific talents, abilities, and experiences gained throughout their lifetime. Their own core values, purpose, and culture began developing in their earliest encounters with others, and are impacted in each stage of life. It is a life-long process of discovery and rediscovery.

Bridging Culture Begins in Childhood

My first exposure to cultural differences began as a child, without my awareness.

When we're young, every sound, voice, accent, and habit is both foreign and familiar. Initially, they're foreign because everything is new. With continued exposure and repetition, they become familiar. Having not yet learned or been exposed to what is "normal" for our regional location, exposure is built on a familial basis until we're old enough to branch out into the world with whatever societal norms are built into our existence.

As the youngest of six children, in a large multinational family, bridging culture was a regular occurrence. I didn't view my grandma's Belgian accent as an accent, it was a natural sound to my ears, just as her Belgian recipes were natural to my sense of taste. Her Lukken cookies were incredible and I was eager to help roll balls of dough and eat cookies warm off the press, or after they had chilled into their crisp snowflake shapes. She came to this country as a teenager, and utilized her sewing skills as a job and a craft. The clothes she created for me and my dolls were unlike anything that could be found on the store shelves.

My Italian great-grandmother, Granny, had an entirely different sound and style that was as familiar and delightful as whatever was on the stove or baking in the oven when we arrived at her house for a visit. It wasn't until I was older that I even recognized my relatives had accents, nor did it matter. What mattered to me was the warmth, kindness, good food, and hugs. No one spoke of nationalities at the time, they were simply family with interesting stories and diverse contributions we were accustomed to. During an elementary school project, I learned I had four nationalities to choose from to write a heritage report on, and thus a new level of awareness began.

When we grew up enough to venture outside of our houses, a whole different array of sounds, voices, accents, and habits came to our attention. My neighborhood friends had different names for their grandparents: Situ, Jiddo, Nonna, Oma, the list went on. It was no different to us than the first or last names of our friends, or the names of our streets growing up. We played on neighborhood porches and backyards as though they were family during our outdoor games; these experiences and values took precedence over the outside world.

Year by year, we moved out of our regional understanding and learned more formally about different cultures. Our landscape extended more in college. Cultural diversity took on a whole new meaning with exposure to students and professors from different countries, religions, and economic brackets combined with our academic studies and group projects. We learned to ask better questions and listen intently to our teammates' answers in order to pull together assignments in a way that would elicit the highest grades. It was a helpful transition to the corporate world where, soon, our borders were to open even further with vendors, clients, and partners from around the globe.

Welcome to the Multicultural and Multigenerational Workplace

In most facets of life, effective teamwork is integral to success. If we remain cognizant of the lessons from our childhood families, neighborhoods, sports, and school experiences we're attuned to the concept that people matter and seek to build diverse teams with a variety of skills and abilities. In order to maximize our effectiveness, it is imperative to extend our company culture and connect with the individuals' cultural differences and connections.

Defining *"culture"* as a noun, according to Merriam-Webster:

- the customary beliefs, social forms, and material traits of a racial, religious, or social group
- the set of shared attitudes, values, goals, and practices that characterizes an institution or organization
- the set of values, conventions, or social practices associated with a particular field, activity, or societal characteristic
- the integrated pattern of human knowledge, belief, and behavior that depends upon the capacity for learning and transmitting knowledge to succeeding generations"[2]

Recognizing and establishing the culture your company wants to embody requires some introspection before disseminating it throughout the ranks. It is helpful to start with the core leadership team to establish a baseline understanding of the core "What, Why, When, Where, and How." The first step is for the company to clearly understand its own unique makeup of why they exist. The mission and vision must be clarified in a way that can be easily expressed and remembered.

It is then essential to define and integrate values into the core of the company. Authentic, values-based decision-making becomes the new predecessor for how to communicate and measure success. Depending on the size and breadth of the organization, it can remain at the core leadership level or it may be extended to involve employees representing different facets and/or locations of the business. Having an outside facilitator can help with both the brainstorming process, and then narrowing down to what resonates utilizing a more holistic and unbiased view.

While determining your core values, ask a few key questions:

1. What does success look like on a daily, weekly, and monthly basis?
2. What values are present in these successes?
3. What does failure look like, or what is an unfavorable experience?
4. What values are missing in these unfavorable experiences?
5. What values are crucial and must be present?

Once defined, the fundamental components of mission, vision, voice, and values cannot be taken for granted. Certainly, it helps to publish this key information for your employees, vendors, partners, and clients to see on your website and in publications. However, words alone will not bring them to life as living elements of your brand. As the organization inevitably grows and changes, the quandary of how to maintain or evolve the culture can become a challenge if not given adequate attention and focus in order to perpetuate a successful transition.

How can we make sure all of the staff and clients truly see and understand our culture? Leaders must learn how to communicate, hire, and measure talent in a way that aligns with their values in order to improve the employee experience and create an ideal culture where the battle for talent will be won. Success can be found within a culture where people want to "co-brand" and identify with the company values while preserving their own unique make-up.

In order to actualize culture we must develop a greater respect for the intricacies of our employees themselves in order to optimize our team. Each member of the team has individual gifts and a sense of purpose that reflects their own experiences and values. No matter how great our ideas and technology, it is the combination and curation of the people on our team(s) that can help guide our overall strategic and cultural development.

While the customer experience and optimizing profits remain important, in today's landscape, the employee experience must be considered a vital part of the process itself. How do their own values align with the company's? What energizes and de-energizes them? What information do they need to do their job more effectively? What unique experiences can they contribute to brainstorming exercises as we work together to create tomorrow's success stories? This new and valuable set of ingredients can be added to the appraisal process, literally bridging team values into team victories.

Extending CULTURE and Building the Bridge

A company is only as strong as its team, and there are certain elements required to build an effective cultural bridge.

- Communication
- Understanding
- Leadership
- Trust
- Unity
- Respect
- Energy

As you seek to unleash the full potential of your organization, **COMMUNICATION** is the most foundational element for productive teams and human connection. Certainly, it helps for the whole team to understand the mission, vision, and values of the organization beyond a few written words. It must literally be built into the voice of the company and propagated throughout all levels of decision-making. If communicated effectively, there will be no question as to how to proceed on challenging and day-to-day decisions when the values themselves become living and known elements of the organization.

"We've developed the mission, vision, and values; now, how do we communicate them to the team?"

First, let's start by switching out one word ... not **TO** the team, but **WITH** the team. Celebrate the opportunity to transmit and receive information, while opening the door to impact or change. It is important to develop a bi-directional communication strategy of sharing information about the intentions, or shifts in strategy, with the teams. You must then remain open to listening to how these shifts impact each party. This offers a more effective way of creating team engagement in solutions. If possible, allow space to develop multigenerational teams to bolster each other's understanding of how to brainstorm with less judgment and a more open forum of understanding.

Perhaps music can be utilized as the common ground and as a reminder that each generation has experienced rifts in understanding when it came to the popular music of their time. At some point, they, too, may have challenged the status quo. Encourage each member of the team to take the stage and have a voice. Together the experience has more depth and dimension and can create a new understanding that exceeds each one alone.

Strategically, it is helpful to reinforce values in your policies and procedures. Document standards and create an evaluation system to help make it obvious when decisions are in alignment with the team culture. Then, translate complex concepts in a simpler fashion (simplify and humanize). The results can manifest into a set of clear communication tools to help with critical decisions and discussions. These tools will offer more intentionality and **UNDERSTANDING** of how and why decisions are made and can be used to guide your organization as you live your values, activate your purpose and uphold your brand promise.

"You will know it when you see it, and you will know it when you don't."

This open forum of understanding enables each member of the team to take on a **LEADERSHIP** position of their own. Leadership becomes redefined with regard to influence and choice, rather than a title alone. Anyone can choose to lead, regardless of their position. The door to lead opens with communication, understanding, and clarity. In order to lead with confidence, however, a level of **TRUST** must be built through expression and collaboration. The barometer for trust and credibility is measured with a key question:

Is the organization **LIVING** *its values?*

When a company lives its values, employees, clients, and partners will know what to expect with day-to-day decisions and circumstances. There is a confluence of intentions. When a company does not live its values, the level of trust dissipates, and conflict is given fertile ground to proliferate.

Here are a few examples of value misalignment:

- INTEGRITY, but asking employees to lie.
- JOY, without taking time to celebrate small victories.
- COMPASSION, but being too busy to listen to employee or client concerns.
- RESPECT, but without a diversity, equity, inclusion, and belonging program in place.
- AUTHENTICITY, but not living in accordance with the mission, vision, and values.

Culture needs to be consistent and encouraged in ways that are constructive and productive, not simply on a graphic or website. This level of consistency brings a level of **UNITY** as it is built into business decisions, performance metrics, and messaging. It can then be utilized as a compass to navigate the day-to-day challenges and achievements. The team is brought together for one purpose and is "in the know" already. They understand the "What, Why, When, Where, and How" without having to know every detail of every particular instance. There are many ways to accomplish a goal, but first, the team must agree on the problem they're trying to solve and the end goal they're trying to achieve. When we combine our talents with others, we are capable of anything, as there is strength in service to our purpose. This blend of living values is a reminder they can count on, amplify, and evangelize.

Bridging culture within an organization can have a warmer feel by remembering each team member matters and is valuable to the output of the whole. No one is better than another; they are simply different. Reframing success by having **RESPECT** for each role in bringing your product, service, or program to market helps to leverage the full team. From the person on the receiving dock to the salesperson who landed the deal, storytelling can feature a multitude of characters and storylines to ultimately celebrate the team's victories. When values are alive, as part of the lifeblood of the organization or team, there is a focus, integration, and an unbeatable **ENERGY** transmitted throughout the organization with both challenges and achievements.

An Example of Living Your Values While Bridging Culture

Early in my career, I worked in operations with the factory. Initially, I was the Supply Chain cog of the wheel. I aligned material requirements in order to meet production schedules and fill customer orders. That cog became part of the team the day I walked out on the factory floor to learn more about my internal customer, the factory, while inquiring about their concerns before changing production plans. Our decision-making process shifted to a bi-directional conversation about potential impacts prior to making a commitment to our Account Teams. Each major shift became an open conversation as we shared information about potential changes to our production plan, asked opinions about the impacts, and embraced ideas for how to achieve the goals of our customers and market demands. Together, with the factory and the industrial engineering team, we responded to our customer needs with zero delinquencies while also enduring ever-changing technology and market pressures.

It was imperative for the factory and industrial engineering team to learn about my own intentions and the reasons behind them as well as for me to learn about their needs and the impact of change on their situation so we could work on solutions together. Our team dynamic didn't end there. As the Supply Chain side of the business, my team extended to work with upper management, sales, finance, and the Japanese program teams to ensure the $3.5 billion contract was met with impeccable respect for the needs of the customer. An ongoing negotiation was needed at times to understand what was essential vs. desired. The key to success was understanding the difference, and responding in a way that would minimize expenses while maximizing the bottom line for all parties considered. It was essential to understand the culture and values of the customer and to respond in a way that honored both.

In order to effectively work with our Japanese customers, we were immersed in a culture class prior to our travels. Gaining a greater understanding of symbol culture and non-verbal communication was helpful for us to comprehend the significance of certain gestures, such as how we accepted a business card, to nodding and bowing. In addition, we learned how some verbal responses are often misinterpreted. "Hai" is stated as a way of saying "I hear you – I may or may not agree"... not necessarily "Yes." While "Very difficult" and/or a deep inhale often meant "absolutely not." By gaining a greater understanding of common responses, both sides were often saved months of time and cost by not misinterpreting their, and our, intentions.

When we visited Japan for a series of field installations, our team was paired with Japanese equivalents for each role to help get product in the country and out to the field. For a month, our teams leveraged one another's skills and abilities to successfully troubleshoot challenges and install the product. While our methodologies were different, we were equally respectful of the others' processes. The clock on my office wall, gifted from a Japanese colleague, is a reminder of the shared experience and how it's always time to cultivate respect.

Full Team Ahead

Most people want to solve problems, connect with others, and discover new solutions. As we uncover and define key strategies to motivate and engage your company culture, you're in a better position to move your company "Full Team Ahead."

As you seek to move forward, **SIMPLIFY** the components of your intentions. Bring in your core values to listen and **HUMANIZE** the response with a greater context of understanding and compassion. Then, move to **AMPLIFY** the offering in a way where all parties feel seen, heard, and understood. The shift to **EVANGELIZE** the solutions becomes natural as the team expands to your partners and to the customer itself. The customer becomes as much a part of the team as you are, with the same core acceptance and understanding of their unique contributions and needs. Believe in who you are, what you're doing, why you're doing it, and where you need to be, and then listen – *really listen* – to your employees and customers to produce the success you're dreaming of.

The team is valued as they are seen, heard, understood, and brought into a sense of inclusion and belonging missing from other experiences. When a mission, vision, and values are pushed onto a team, they can be difficult to embrace. But when a mission, vision, and values are explained and given space for retrospection and inclusion in the process, the door opens to more. The door opens to uplift the voices of the team by embracing and accepting their own concerns and creativity. No longer is it simply one mission, vision, and values, but rather a collective of interests weaving together with a common purpose. The threads expand into a tapestry of possibility, and the integration broadens possibility beyond the initial vision of *one*.

Multicultural and multigenerational inclusion can become an inherent part of the solution to whatever challenges you might face as a company. When each person is valued for who they actually are, they become part of something more. The collective creativity lifts the energy to move beyond an idea or vision to an endless array of potential impacts. Individually sparked, but collectively inspired. It's time to move "Full Team Ahead."

Notes

1. Ballas, Jillian. Generation. Accessed 24 May 2023.
2. Merriam-Webster. Culture. Accessed 14 April 2023

Susan LePlae Miller

Susan LePlae Miller is a business consultant, coach, speaker and poet who helps you realize your vision by recognizing and releasing your team's potential. She partners with a global community to deliver compassionate care and values throughout her process of transformation.

As Founder of Pieces of I, LLC, Susan integrates the mission, vision, and values within your team to help maximize your impact. By embracing diversity, she helps utilize team members' unique passions, values, and abilities in a way to help overcome challenges and accomplish objectives.

With a strong background in Operations (Partnerships, Product, and Supply Chain Management), Susan understands the inner workings of business and how teamwork and collaboration fuels results.

Susan is also the Vice President of Partnerships and Programs at My Density Matters, a breast cancer nonprofit, where she has helped build and develop international partnerships with and programs to over 40 countries on 6 continents with health equity as a primary driver to inspire early diagnosis and self-advocacy.

Susan is co-author of Mission Hope: Thriving Through Seasons of the Soul, stories of HOPE and rising above life's challenges and adversities, a Featured Contributor at BizCatalyst360°, and an avid content creator on LinkedIn.

How can Susan add value to your organization?

- Strategic Consulting
- Mental Fitness Coaching
- Team Workshops

Susan's personal why is to "Value each person for who they actually are" and her life mantra is to "Know your value, Live your values".

Connect with Susan LePlae Miller:

LinkedIn: https://www.linkedin.com/in/susan-leplae-miller/

Website: www.piecesofi.com

Pieces of I, LLC on LinkedIn: https://www.linkedin.com/company/64989017/

Facebook: https://www.facebook.com/piecesofi

Instagram: https://www.instagram.com/piecesofillc/

Twitter: https://twitter.com/PiecesofI

YouTube: https://www.youtube.com/@PiecesOfI

IO.

Impactful Leadership

Driving Culture in a New Era

Tiersa Hall | World Class Master Trainer, HR & Culture Consultant, and Leadership and Engagement Coach

James was an extremely successful Division Head. When it came to operations, he simply thrived. All year-end projected budgets for his department were often surpassed, some by as high as 20%. It was undeniably evident to his colleagues that James had solid team members working in his field. During his six-year stint working, he never missed a targeted goal...until recently. He went from consistently hitting goals to merely hitting budgets to, for the first time in his career, failing to meet one. This was devastating for James because he honestly felt, in terms of leadership and operational approach, that he wasn't doing anything outside of his normal formula for success.

So, what changed? In using my Senior HR Experience to help James we peeled back the layers and uncovered several key observations. Firstly, James lost several of his high performers. Exit interviews from those performers revealed lack of emotional connection and loyalty to their current role, but it also highlighted one of his most efficient team members who had a newfound value for work-life balance and wanted to explore more flexible hours. She never requested better work-life balance or flexible hours; she felt she wouldn't be granted these things based on the type of person she knew her manager to be. Another high performer's exit interview illustrated a move to an organization who's culture and brand that aligned with her needs.

What I found to be most telling was my-one-on-one assessment interview with James. When I asked how he kept his team motivated his responses seemed more linked to consequences for when a goal was not met. He painted a picture of a very structured style and restrictions that allowed for little to no deviation. James was a brilliant manager who had great processes. However, he had minimal human connection in his relationships, and because humans are psychologically inclined to establish a greater sense of loyalty to humans than tasks, he (like many other managers in current times) are experiencing challenges with turnover and employee satisfaction.

According to a 2022 EY U.S. Generation survey regarding corporate culture, "more than 90% of employees self-reported that culture impacts their decision to stay with their company."[1]

Today's Culture is more richly diverse than it has ever been. This, coupled with recent world-changing events, has forever shaped the world of work we now live in. The player's advantage has shifted. It has now been placed squarely in the hands of the employee. An employee who once obediently followed the status quo, but now seeks to enter into the equation, demands for inclusion that speaks to their individual needs. Employees actively seek needs such as support, belonging, mutual understanding, and flexibility. To put it plainly: people want more. These are no longer simple requests; they have become non-negotiable and direct factors in retention and the stability of organizations around the world.

We are in a new era of business and the workforce; for the first time in history, we have five generations in the workplace simultaneously. These include:

- The Silent Generation,
- Baby Boomers,
- Generation-X
- Millennials, and
- Generation-Z

Each generation brings with them different expectations, traditions, and mindsets. Many of which are continuously evolving.

Baby Boomers are not as aligned with the company's culture, with less than 30% saying culture didn't have much impact on their remaining at the organization. On the other side of the generational spectrum, the workforce of the future – Gen-Z and Millennials – report that culture plays a big part in their intent to stay with their employer, at nearly 40% for the two groups.

Remote and hybrid work structures have further added more complexity to the already moving targets that are work structures.

So, what does this mean for the leaders of today? It means that getting by with hard-shaped leadership styles has become futile. In order to drive culture, leaders of today need to be relevant with the times, well-rounded, and most of all, they need to adapt the philosophy of building impactful relationships.

You may be wondering what exactly an impactful relationship is.

Impactful relationships are ones that are primarily motivated by a leader's desire to connect and drive growth within their team members in a deep and purposeful way. This is achieved through personalization, communication, and greater knowledge of self.

Rather than shaping others using company standards or expectations, they strive to meet people where they are and use the discoveries from those meetings to help shape the relationship. This unlocks a great power in influence and a greater ability to connect to and drive culture well.

The key elements of an Impactful Leadership lie within its name. One three-syllable word that will help light the path to the future of culture impact- IMPACTFUL.

~ IM ~

Knowing yourself is the beginning of wisdom – Aristotle

The first two letters in the word IMPACTFUL are "IM" and they are very powerful. The "I" speaks to identifying and the "M" represents ME or Myself.

When someone says I AM it is usually associated with a strong sense of clarity. Impactful relationships start with a leader having a clear and accurate breakdown of who he or she is.

A leader should test self-knowledge by asking himself these questions:

- "Do I know who I am?" (Personal)
- "What do others think I am?" (Your Team)
- "What does my company culture require me to be?" (Your Organization)

Let's do some self-reflection. If I were to ask you if you consider yourself a good leader, what would you say? How would that (I **AM** a good leader) be measured? The truth is that most leaders naturally see themselves in a positive light. After all, viewing themselves positively may be the only reason they continue to lead.

I recall a Senior Executive who came to see me during my time as an HR Director. She was expressing her frustration at recent behavior changes in one of her team members. This Senior Executive inquired what was wrong with her team member, but received no reason or response to the question. Little did she know that the same team member in question had come to see me and identified that same Senior Executive as the person culpable for their frustration. This Senior Executive had wracked her brain, sharing with me countless scenarios of what she thought could be wrong. Never once did she consider herself. This was a learning moment for both of us. From that experience, I formulated this quote that I use with clients to this day: Leadership 101 "*When trying to identify a potential challenge or area of concern, never forget to consider that it just might be you.*"

There are times where we as leaders are unaware of our own shortcomings. When we are not in tune, we can inadvertently contribute to a toxic work environment. Once, I was conducting a two-day workshop with leaders, and I asked them all what they thought of toxic leaders. Everyone in the room agreed that they have no place in the working environment. However, through weeks of coaching, quite a few had behaviors that contributed to the toxic spaces they were working in.

A Self Awareness Study was conducted by Emotional Intelligence Expert and Harvard Business Review Researcher Tasha Euric. Across the studies they identified that self-awareness had two forms:

They categorized the first as *internal self-awareness*. This represents how clearly we see our own values, passions, and aspirations fitting with our environment, reactions (including thoughts, feelings, behaviors, strengths, and weaknesses), and impact on others. Persons with this quality tend to have a higher job and relationship satisfaction, personal and social control, and happiness; it is negatively related to anxiety, stress, and depression.

They categorized the second as *external self-awareness*. This means understanding how other people view us, in terms of those same factors listed above. The research revealed that people who know how others see them are more skilled at showing empathy and taking others' perspectives. For leaders who see themselves as their employees do, their employees tend to have a better relationship with them, feel more satisfied with them, and see them as more effective in general.[2]

The study went on to test in order to determine how many leaders possessed both forms of awareness. Here is what they concluded: "Only 10%–15% of the people studied actually fit the criteria for both levels of awareness."

What these statistics tell us is that awareness is beyond our own individualistic thinking and that, quite often and despite having the best intentions, we can still make indecorous decisions in communication and in leading those whom we are responsible for.[3]

The Four Self-Awareness Archetypes

This 2x2 maps internal self-awareness (how well you know yourself) against external self-awareness (how well you understand how others see you).

	EXTERNAL SELF-AWARENESS
Introspectors	**Aware**
They're clear on who they are but don't challenge their own views or search for blind spots by getting feedback from others. This can harm their relationships and limit their success.	They know who they are, what they want to accomplish, and seek out and value others' opinions. This is where leaders begin to fully realize the true benefits of self-awareness.
Seekers	**Pleasers**
They don't yet know who they are, what they stand for, or how their teams see them. As a result, they might feel stuck or frustrated with their performance and relationships.	They can be so focused on appearing a certain way to others that they could be overlooking what matters to them. Over time, they tend to make choices that aren't in service of their own success and fulfillment.

INTERNAL SELF-AWARENESS ↑ HIGH ↓ LOW

LOW ← EXTERNAL SELF-AWARENESS → HIGH

⊽ HBR

So, how do we as leaders increase our level of awareness to better understand who we are and how that understanding affects others? A leadership or personality assessment does wonders in discovering this.

As a Certified Maxwell DISC Behavioral Consultant who has conducted hundreds of assessments, I have seen the impact first-hand. What is particularly effective about this assessment is that it is captured through graphing three key areas:

- The first is the *"public self"* (the mask) which is how others see you as a leader
- The *"private self"* (the core), which identifies how you are most likely to respond when in stress or tense environments
- The *"perceived self"* (the mirror) which is the manner in which you perceive your typical behavior; in other words, your self-perception. This graph is usually able to capture the behaviors that we use with other people as a leader that we may be unaware of and reflects the typical approach.

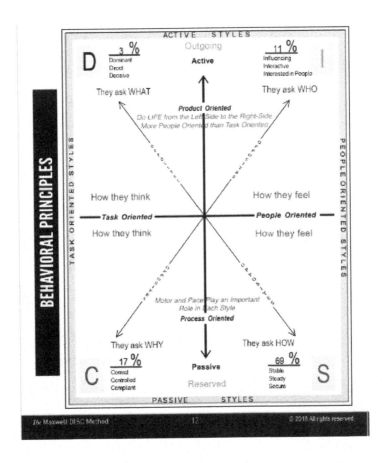

During one of our coaching sessions, Susan, a Corporate Executive, began to share how things had been going with her team. She had mostly positive things to say about the team; however, there was one team member with whom she felt there wasn't much engagement and connection. She tried making small talk and was ignored. She offered invites to social events that were declined. She also expressed that when it came to criticism the individual in question was not receptive and a simple coaching moment always turned out to be an email war. I encouraged her to do an assessment for herself and her team and, as a result, several light bulbs turned on.

First, she learned that her personality type had a view of importance as "people-first" "tasks second" view of importance. Jill, the team member she had a lack of connection with, was conversely "task first," "people second." This explained why the social event invitations were declined. Sarah was scheduling many of them during the middle of the day. Jill's personality didn't feel fulfilled leaving work behind. When it came to the coaching moment(s) turned into "email wars," Sarah also learned that Jill's biggest fear (based on her personality type) was criticism. So, having an in-person conversation would have been more effective than an email where tones can be misunderstood and thus intentions and situations misinterpreted.

The findings from the assessment didn't change who Sarah or Jill were, but what it did do was open up a greater understanding of the why behind their actions. These discoveries allowed Sarah, as the leader, to make adjustments to her own misplaced emotions as well as adjust her management style to meet Jill in a familiar space that resonated with who she was. From there, she was able to build a solid connection with Jill while recognizing and celebrating the strengths she brought to the team along the way. A clear understanding of self and others allows for transparency helps Conflict Management and makes having difficult conversations far more manageable.

Once we, as leaders, have a clear view of who our team members are and gain better awareness of our team members and how they read us, we have another task at hand. We then must gain a clear understanding of how our truest self fits into the organizational culture of the organization. After all, we can't drive a connection that we cannot see.

A great place to start is with a revisit of the organization's Mission statement. This is an excellent place to stay because this is *why* the company seeks to exist. Does it resonate naturally with who you are and how comfortable you are guiding your team towards this purpose?

Core values are deeply connected to behavioral traits. We have read and learned core values of the organizations throughout our career, but how often do we consider how they tie into our own values? In light of this, I often ask client leaders that are experiencing a disconnect and considering leaving the company they work for to look at the organization's core values; provided that they are being practiced within the organization and not existing symbolically. I then have them underline the ones that speak directly to what they personally value. The greater the common ground of shared values the easier it is for the leader to live out the expectations.

The organization's culture requires us, as leaders, to be unified with the values, mission, and even the vision of plans for the future. If these elements do not match or have much common ground, a leader should see this as a direct threat to the full extent of productivity at work and either attempt to impact the culture to change or consider the pursuit of a better match.

When we combine the powers of knowledge of self with the knowledge of others and align ourselves with the organization's culture we can gain so much and benefit greatly. Our capacity to influence increases and we can confidently communicate without fear to make the commitments needed to drive the culture forward.

~ PACT ~

"If you make a decision, a pact with someone, you should say, 'I'm gonna do this,' and you should stick to it." – Erykah Badu

The word PACT lies in the very center of Impactful. This is the phase where the culture is reshaped and trust along with expectations are established. In this phase, leaders ask themselves:

- "What commitment am I willing to make?"
- "What agreement do I need to foster with my team?
- "What expectations will I honor?"

It is so easy to say to ourselves that we will endeavor to

become better leaders to our teams. When we choose to voice that, it is given true power. It gives leaders accountability to deliver on the promises made. It is a manifestation of what we would like to see happen.

Merriam-Webster Dictionary defines a pact as:

- "any solemn agreement or promise between two or more people;"[4]

To take this further, solemn is characterized by "deep sincerity." Every commitment should begin with sincerity. There must be a genuine and innate desire to not only make a commitment but to also hold true to it. If we don't value the commitment, the motivation to keep it will diminish and we will fail.

Voicing a commitment also prompts within us to the need to be vulnerable. When I started the journey of leadership, I felt this immense pressure to always be right and never make mistakes. If I had made mistakes, I wouldn't admit to them. I have discovered great power in vulnerability because as a leader falls, his team's true strength rises.

I recall early in my career a time that we were considering the implications of implementing new systems. Being a natural, people-oriented individual, this was where I thrived. When it came to processes and precision, I knew the basics; but it wasn't an area high on my list of excelling, nor was it a desire for me. Being aware of the direction that the organization was going in, I sourced the right talent to fill the gap so that the organization could get maximum results in that area. As the leader of that team, I felt compelled to always have the answers.

Weeks earlier, I had voiced a commitment to the newly constructed team to be more transparent and encouraged *them* to be transparent in their efforts, failures, and need for help. I had a recommendation: I had to make a major decision for the direction of processes. I had requested recommendations from my expert hire but the stellar information she gave was difficult to garner deep understanding. So, we were presented with an opportunity to stand true to the commitment I had made. I had to admit that I had no clue of the terminology used in this situation; and while I closed my eyes waiting for the impact of, "You should know this," I was met with support, and a desire to be taught. I also realized that this was an opportunity for my team member to thrive and a proud moment to realize their value in the team. Through growth and experience, what I realized was this: the more transparent I was with my team, even in my shortcomings and errors, the greater the impact on our relationship. From there, we created a culture where the celebrations of strengths were upheld. Had I not made that commitment of transparency, I'm not sure how open or comfortable I would have been to admit that shortcoming (not knowing the terminology); which ultimately led to such a great milestone in the growth of our team.

Commitment doesn't equal perfect execution, but it

means we vow to be perfect in our intention and our efforts.

One of the best support systems for the pact or commitment you make is to create an environment where there is opportunity for transparency. Throughout more than sixteen years of HR work and as a Master Trainer, one of the biggest observed challenges for leaders has been confrontation and communication. This includes creating social spaces and opportunities within the work hours for team members to share how they are feeling or give insight. It also might involve finding creative ways to secure the mindset, keeping the intentional thoughts flowing daily, using engagement tools that spark conversations, and getting team members engaged throughout their work week.

> Commit to ensuring the representation of diversity of your team. Culture must be multi-dynamic. Diverse personalities will have different expectations.

Once commitment is made, leaders should focus on getting buy-in from the team. In other words: you must turn your time and attention toward team members on board with the chosen commitment. Confirming the commitment you have offered ensures that the accuracy of the insight you have derived from your beginning phase holds true to the actual needs of your team. Getting buy-in goes beyond presenting the commitment in a general meeting. Now that you know the behavior and personality traits of your team, you need to create several methods of communication to ensure each member is reached.

Finally, commitment must also be connected to the final element of the Pact stage which is alignment with the company culture. Leaders should build along with their teams standards that represent and resonate with existing company culture and identity. The day to day tasks and responsibilities performed should be clear examples illustrated and connected to company culture that each team member will contribute and commit to. This feeds a sense of pride and ownership amongst team members who will now be support systems to the leader in achieving high productivity levels as well as a healthy work culture.

~ FUL ~

Our fulfillment is not in our isolated human grandeur, but in our intimacy with the larger earth community, for this is also the larger dimension of our being. –
Thomas Berry

It is of no coincidence that the F-U-L comes at the end of Impact. According to Cambridge University, impact is defined as: "having the stated quality to a high degree."[5] During this phase, impact is magnified at its highest levels. Leaders have explored who they are individually, committed to their teams, and achieved buy-in. Now they have come full circle with their team with a clear identity and platform commitment to work from.

Here is what I call my FULosophy:

FUL – A *Fulfilled Leader* +*Fulfilled Employees* = *Maximized Sense of belonging*

If you were challenged to recall every instance where you were included or involved in an activity or initiative, many of you would not be able to do so. This is because it has either happened quite often or it is an innate expectation that we have as humans to be involved and take part in team-oriented or people-centric activities. However, what about the times where you have not been included? We remember them – the disappointment, the hurt, the feeling of isolation. We question if what we have contributed has been that insignificant that it would cause us to be forgotten. We ask ourselves if we are in the right place, whether we truly belong in this group, in this community, or in this workspace. This doesn't even begin to mention what it can do to the self-esteem of those impacted. You see the feeling of being excluded is far more reaching and longer lasting and many of those emotions show themselves at work.

The phrase "sense of belonging" is often seen as a fluffy, flowery concept – why? This is because, more often than not, there has been a great challenge to measure human behavior in the workplace. However, in this new era, and following a pandemic wave, organizations have at their fingertips technology and software that can capture the impact of truly understanding and working with human behavior and forging connections in mind.

So, how does sense of belonging impact business positively?

A study was conducted by behavioral scientists at BetterUp, and data revealed that "if workers feel like they belong, companies reaped substantial bottom-line benefits. High belonging was linked to a whopping 56% increase in job performance, a 50% drop in turnover risk, and a 75% reduction in sick days. For a 10,000-person company, this would result in annual savings of more than $52M."[6]

Further, employees with higher workplace belonging also showed a 167% increase in their employer promoter score (their willingness to recommend their company to others). They also received double the raises, and 18 times more promotions.[7]

In coaching organizations seeking to impact culture through leadership, I often use the analogy of car ownership to drive the concept of a sense of belonging home. Imagine that you were just rewarded with your dream car. You have been driving it for two weeks. I imagine at this stage, you are taking care of it. You're washing it, regularly keeping your tank filled (at least a quarter of the way, right?), and being very cautious around corners and in parking lots. Now, you have to go out of town and one of your siblings or spouse has to drive it. Will they exercise the same amount of care? What state is your vehicle returned to you in? Most often the responses are, "The vehicle is dirty, there's no gas in the tank," or maybe even "There's a dent or bumper scratch."

So, why is the care so much different? It is because the car belongs to **you**. We tend to be more invested in the things that belong or that we **FEEL** belong to us. Employees need to feel a sense of belonging and ownership in the organization that they are a part of. They need to see their value and the space they are to fill.

When a leader's team members are led with full impact, their eyes and ears are wide open to be taught to be guided. You are gassed up and ready to drive the culture.

And your legacy will show it. As an impactful leader, your deliberate intention and commitment to meet and lead people where they are will pave the way for those you lead, building a better future. Impactful leaders will do wonders in transformation for the organization that will benefit.

Of course, driving the culture doesn't mean disregarding your operational goals. After all, operations will still need to be managed; but I'm confident that if we lead IM-PACT-FULLY, it will make the journey of driving culture that much easier.

Culture is often considered as a broad concept – something that everyone in the organization does together. However as we have seen here, leaders are the main drivers of the culture and the effective driving of a culture requires us to dig deep beyond the surface of the organization, pass the needs of ourselves, to embrace a team where they are, and foster a new journey together.

As fellow optimist and thought leader, Simon Sinek, put it: "A *culture is strong when people work with each other, for each other. A culture is weak when people work against each other, for themselves.*"

May we as leaders graciously accept the challenge to innovate ourselves so that we can effectively lead and drive culture in this ever-evolving, new era.

Notes

1. Americas, EY. "2022 EY US Generation Survey Reveals Impact Company Culture Plays in Employee Retention." EY, 13 Oct. 2022, www.ey.com/en_us/news/2022/10/ey-generation-survey-reveals-impact-company-culture-plays-in-employee-retention.

2. Eurich, Tasha. "What Self-Awareness Really Is (and How to Cultivate It)." Harvard Business Review, 6 Apr. 2023, hbr.org/2018/01/what-self-awareness-really-is-and-how-to-cultivate-it.

3. Okpara, Atuma, and Agwu M Edwin. "Self-Awareness and Organizational Performance." European Journal of Research and Reflection in Management Sciences Vol. 3 No. 1, 2015, www.idpublications.org/wp-content/uploads/2014/12/Self-Awareness-and-Organizational-performance-Full-Paper.pdf. Accessed 24 May 2023.

4. https://www.merriam-webster.com/dictionary/pact

5. "Powerful Diversity Workplace Statistics to Know for 2023." InStride, www.instride.com/insights/workplace-diversity-

and-inclusion-statistics/. Accessed 24 May 2023.

6. Johnson, Whitney, et al. "The Value of Belonging at Work."
   Harvard Business Review, 21 Dec. 2021, hbr.org/2019/12/the-
   value-of-belonging-at-work.

7. Skerik, Sarah. "Good Reads: Belonging in the Workplace."
   Engagement Multiplier, 12 Oct. 2021,
   www.engagementmultiplier.com/resources/good-reads-
   belonging-in-the-
   workplace/#:~:text=%E2%80%9CIf%20workers%20feel%20li
   ke%20they,of%20more%20than%20%2452M.

Tiersa Hall

Tiersa is a World Class Master Trainer, HR & Culture Consultant, and Leadership and Engagement Coach. Through her company Impactful Imprints Training & Consulting, she helps professionals and organizations and bridge the gap between where they are and where they want to be by maximizing leadership, increasing engagement, and fostering healthy work cultures.

With over 16 years of experience in Leadership, Hospitality, and Human Resources, Tiersa has served as an HR Strategist to high-end luxury resorts in the Turks and Caicos and has mastered the art of communication, building trusted, quality relationships with professionals and organizations grounded in respect.

Carrying the title of Certified Senior HR Professional (SPHR) and a Certified Master Trainer with the Association of

Talent Development (ATD), Tiersa is also an accomplished writer and has penned over 40 articles for Forbes on topics ranging from Human Resources, Work Cultures, Employee Engagement, and Leadership. She is also Certified DISC Behavioural Consultant with the John Maxwell Team.

Serving as a Lead Consultant for Cultural Transformations in the Caribbean Region and beyond, Tiersa helps organizations structure and revamp their company culture and get team buy-in, as well as tackle toxic areas in their work environment. For this and much more, Forbes selected Tiersa as the Leader of The Healthy Work Cultures for the Forbes Human Resources Council 2022-2023.

In her spare time, Tiersa can be found Advocating for Autism, writing poetry, creating fun training and social media content, and spending time with her husband Kaz, son Kade, bonus daughters Genesis and Amazingly Autistic Twins Brooklyn & Lyric.

Mom, Wife, Entrepreneur, and Speaker, Tiersa has countless stories of defying the odds, discovering purpose, and leading others to greatness. She remains committed to maximizing leadership, increasing engagement, and fostering healthy work environments, one culture at a time!

How can Tiersa add value to your organization?

- Workshops & Training
- Keynote Speaking
- Executive & Company Coaching

- HR Consulting
- Culture Transformations
- Client and Customer Engagement

Connect with Tiersa Hall:

LinkedIn: https://www.linkedin.com/in/tiersahall/

Email: thall@tiersahall.com

Website: www.tiersahall.com

Phone Number: (954-701-8236)

Instagram: https://www.instagram.com/tiersahall/

Facebook: https://www.facebook.com/tiersahall

Tik Tok: https://www.tiktok.com/@tiersahall

II.

Culture Matters

Creating a Culture of Contribution

Elisabeth Galperin | Speaker, Trainer, Coach, Founder & Owner, Peak Productivity

Me: "How's your week going, Ron?"

Ron: "Super busy!"

Me: "How is your family doing, Pam?"

Pam: "Staying busy!"

Me: "What's your week look like, Melissa?"

Melissa: "My schedule is so ridiculously busy!"

It doesn't take much to see the common denominator in all of these verbal exchanges: the word **BUSY**. Take a moment to think about how many times you have likely used this word today, this week, this month. What about the number of times you've heard family, friends, and colleagues talking about being busy, or some version of it, when describing just about every aspect of their life? We talk about being busy ALL. THE. TIME.

Work is busy.

The family is busy.

The weekend is busy.

The grocery store is busy.

The restaurant is busy.

Life is always busy.

You get the point.

Let's face it: we are living in a *culture of busy*. Even when things aren't actually hectic, we sometimes create excess activity ("the busy") because it is so familiar and has become almost comfortable. We turn on the television, start reading celebrity or political news on our phone, turn on the washing machine, and dryer, and the dishwasher, at the same time, then walk outside to mow the lawn. Just another typical Sunday in America; you know, the designated day of rest.

Do any of us actually desire to be busy? Do we wake up each morning and think to ourselves, "I *sure hope I am outrageously busy today!*" I'll be the first to admit, I have normalized being in constant motion – always **doing**, never just **being**. I set a goal last year to adopt the habit of scheduling a time once a week to literally DO NOTHING. That was one of the hardest challenges and most difficult goals I've set for myself in my adult years!

Busy is the new **good**. We often use the word without real intention, without any real meaning behind it. When someone tells us they are "good," do we know anything specific regarding how they are actually doing or feeling? The response, "I'm good" is simply a placeholder in many cases. It has become a way to skirt the truth and to quickly move past the real details of life.

Busy, however, unknowingly sends an unwanted, and often negative, message to others and to ourselves. It has become ingrained in our language. The behaviors this word represents have become the accepted – and often expected – norm in our twenty-first century lives.

The problem with being busy is that it is typically not healthy. Constant busyness is not sustainable. Most important of all, being busy is NOT the same thing as being productive. Is it busyness or is it productivity that our American/workplace/family culture is striving for? 'Busy' as a social status is a problem at many levels, not just for people at a personal level, but for professionals, leaders, and the companies and organizations where we work.

BUSY versus PRODUCTIVE

As a business productivity coach, keynote speaker, and productivity trainer, I interact with professionals of all ages and at varying stages of their careers. Many are managers and leaders in mid-size companies and large corporations. Others are entrepreneurs who are scaling their businesses, growing their teams, and expanding their products and services. ALL of them are sleeping less, working more, and taking on more responsibilities than they can truly handle in the workplace. Why? Because most individuals still believe this is the only, or maybe best, way to climb the ladder in the corporate culture.

I almost always kick off my team trainings and workshops by asking participants to brainstorm a list of synonyms and connotations that come to mind when they see or hear the word BUSY. The responses are almost always the same set of negative words and feelings: stress, overwhelm, disorganization, inefficiency, spinning on a hamster wheel, multi-tasking, feeling out-of-control, whiplash, and chaos.

When I ask the same groups of professionals to reflect upon the word **PRODUCTIVE**, the connotations are much more positive: prioritization, execution, accomplishment, completion, meaningful work, proactive, effectiveness, intentional, and adding value.

One word I rarely hear – yet often suggest and offer to those listening – is what I believe is the driving force and the core human value behind all working professionals' efforts, actions, behaviors and goals: **CONTRIBUTION**.

MISGUIDED FOCUS

There are many theories on why and how American culture – and therefore American companies – erroneously adopted and glorified a culture of busyness. This "idealized" way of living differs drastically from the culture of our ancestors in England and Europe. If we rewind the clock to the late 1800s and early 1900s, and take a look at other cultures, we begin to see that the perception in those days around working hard versus living in leisure was remarkably different. In most of these societies of the past, living in leisure was the true status symbol for wealth, success, intelligence, value, and importance. Anyone who is a fan of Downton Abbey might remember one of Violet Crawley's (the Countess) privileged comments, "What is a weekend?" Set in 1912, she lived a lifestyle where there was no distinction between working days and weekend days for rest. Hard work was done only by members of the lower social classes, people who were presumed to be less intelligent, less important, and frankly, overall *less than.*

Slightly more than 100 years later, the American culture in which we all live and work now glorifies "the hustle and grind." Social status is often now elevated the harder we work, the busier and more overextended we are, the more balls we juggle in the air, and the more obstacles we have to overcome to come out on top. Our culture frequently idolizes the rich and famous who got there by working 80 hour weeks for decades, who prioritized business needs over personal relationships, who gave up and/or lost everything they previously had and valued in order to get to the top of their industry or company. In other words, we now often value and prioritize business over people in order to get to the top of the "wealthiest" or "most successful" lists.

This may sound a bit extreme, but many studies have been conducted to understand Americans' perspectives on people who work hard versus work less. Researchers and authors from the Harvard Business Review presented a short description of a 35-year-old professional named Jeff. Participants in one group were informed that Jeff "works long hours and his calendar is always full." In a second group, participants read that Jeff "does not work and has a leisurely lifestyle." When participants from the two groups were asked to rate the perceived social status of "Jeff," those who saw him as the busier, working man perceived him as higher in status. Studies like this, and several others, have collected data that supports the conclusion that, "the more we believe that one has the opportunity for success based on hard work, the more we tend to think that people who skip leisure and work all the time are of higher standing."[1]

Workplace Culture: Busy vs Productive

"What gets measured gets done."

This statement has resonated with me since the first day I stumbled across it early in my career as a productivity coach and consultant. At the time, I was studying accountability and metrics in the workplace. In researching and observing first-hand the types of metrics that are collected and prioritized – not to mention the metrics that are often absent in work environments – it's no wonder companies are so often cranking out low-quality "busy-work."

The recent news stories on companies that are measuring employee productivity based on mouse-movements or the number of keystrokes per minute make me cringe. Looking at the quantity of emails sent per day or the number of meetings an employee attends per week is simply reinforcement of the obsolescent idea that more is always better.

More and bigger is **not** always better.

Quantity is **rarely** equivalent to quality.

Busy is **not** the same as productivity.

Especially in today's knowledge-based economy.

Where companies are getting it wrong, and perpetuating a negative culture of busyness, is enforcing the antiquated definition of productivity as a measure of output only. These companies are overlooking the fact that activity along with achievement and quality is the true measure of workplace productivity. Busyness is not a value, or a virtue, yet many companies are treating it that way. Consider how many industries and organizations still reward and promote primarily the people who display how "hard" they are working. The legal industry is a great example of where this continues to happen.

Let's analyze a bit further the common perception that to measure an individual's worth and level of contribution to the organization, it is best (and easiest) to look at his/her level of output. Output of energy, information, or product. In reality, the flurry of activity an employee demonstrates may, in fact, be creating a level of chaos and frenzied energy for themselves and for teammates nearby. The busyness is more likely to be indicative of an unhealthy employee. Employees who feel the need to always feel or appear busy are also the individuals who become the most stressed employees. In turn, they then often become physically ill, mentally burnt-out, or emotionally unwell.

Busyness is indeed a health and wellness issue at the personal level. Yet, it is also the health of the company that can become compromised. There is a direct correlation between overworked and overwhelmed employees and a measurable decline in company productivity. A workplace culture of busyness hurts the bottomline. Employees become disengaged, absenteeism increases, and an employee's level of loyalty and commitment to the organization can quickly decline. Research has also proven that companies which overly emphasize, measure, and/or incentivize how much a person works actually results in a drop in productivity levels and efficiency. Employees may be putting in the hours and minutes, according to the clock, but they are likely also producing with less focus, effort, efficiency, and/or effectiveness.

Creating a Culture of Contribution

From quiet quitting (when employees do the bare minimum in their jobs), to quiet constraint (when employees hold on to valuable knowledge at work, rather than sharing it with their colleagues), to whatever the next trend may be, company culture will always be a critical component of every organization that strives to succeed and grow. An organization's culture will need to remain the highest priority for leaders of companies, large and small. A culture left to develop on its own is a culture that will, at best, result in sub-par behaviors, actions, attitudes, and values; at worst, it will be the primary downfall of a company.

The evidence is abundant: a culture of **busy** is clearly not what today's companies and organizations will benefit from, nor is it what they can afford to encourage or allow. A culture focused on **productivity** is much more likely to create a desirable workplace environment. Yet, I would propose that the truly ideal workplace culture – a place where professionals dream of working and where individuals feel extreme gratitude to be a member of the team – is a culture of *contribution*.

- An organization with a culture of contribution has clearly defined the most meaningful tasks and responsibilities for each team member and has created a role in the organization where those activities are prioritized and praised.
- A culture of contribution values each individual's unique skills and strengths, and allows individuals to demonstrate and utilize those skills without placing unreasonable constraints on how long it takes or where work must be completed.
- A culture of contribution provides continuous clarity to each team member regarding how his/her daily tasks are positively impacting and directly contributing to the greater mission, vision, and values of the company.
- A culture of contribution taps into the innate human desire to work at our highest level, put forth our best effort, and contribute in the most significant way possible in order to support the mission and success of the group.

Is this utopia truly attainable? I firmly believe it is.

While the effort to fully change the culture of busyness in America may take another 100 or more years, shifting and transforming the culture as leaders at our organizations can be more quickly and successfully achieved. In all honesty, the steps and shifts suggested below are fairly simple and intuitive. Don't confuse that with "easy." It can be human nature to resist change and keep a firm grasp on what is familiar and what has been the status quo. However, even more powerful than the human need for the safety of the predictable and familiar is the desire to help one's community survive and thrive. Positive social pressure and expectation actually pushes most of us to perform at our best. If you can find a few internal advocates who will help lead the charge, by your side, you will be well on your way towards creating a culture of contribution.

- **Know your team members' S-S-N**: No, not their social security number. From the first day of onboarding, take the time to identify each individual's **strengths**, communication and learning **styles**, and what their greatest **needs** are as it relates to physical working environment, management style, mentoring support, and skills development. It is the simple act of knowing the whole person and understanding how best he/she can contribute to the larger group. You can uncover these important details about each individual through assessments (like DISC, StrengthsFinder, or the Enneagram), internal surveys, skills evaluations, and through good, old-fashioned conversation. Most team members are happy to share what makes them tick when asked from a place of curiosity and authentic interest.

- **Flexibility is Key**: A culture of contribution allows for diversity in individuals. In this post-pandemic world, the culture may also need to integrate hybrid working options for these diverse team members. Some members of the team will be social and extroverted and, therefore, will work best when in the presence of others and in a setting with high activity and energy. Some will be introverted, preferring almost-complete silence and needing a distraction-free space to focus and fully express ideas and creativity. Other team members will produce their highest quality work from 4:00-8:00 AM, while many reach peak productivity levels at 10:00 PM or after. Allow individuals to contribute in their ideal work environments whenever possible. An expectation of conformity has no place in a culture of contribution.
- **Get Specific on Expectations**: A job description or a bulleted list of responsibilities is often vague and written from the 10,000 feet view of a role. As a leader or manager, discuss and define expectations with depth and detail. The reason individuals often default to low-value tasks and "busy work" is because there is often not enough clarity provided regarding how to prioritize, why specific activities are more valuable than others, and how to-do items are connected to the company's success or greater purpose. Make no

assumptions! We've all heard what happens when we ass*u*me, right? Work together with your team members to figure out what deep work versus nonessential tasks looks like for them, then work to eliminate or automate those tasks that are not of high value. Finally, be sure to find out what tasks are most engaging and which are less interesting or even challenging for each individual. Then get creative in finding solutions like re-assigning tasks to others who enjoy the work. Delegate based on interest, skill, and strength versus by title. The seven most dangerous words in business are: ***"We've always done it this way."*** Beware of the tendency to keep a task on someone's plate simply because the previous individual did it and liked to contribute in that way.

- **Use Nontraditional Metrics:** The days of a white board with one large dollar amount as a sales goal for the month are gone. Employees want to know their work is contributing in many additional and different ways than simply towards filling the company's pockets and covering payroll. In a culture of contribution, start by measuring the qualitative, not the quantitative. Prioritize work-life balance. Reward the team member who asked to leave early on a Tuesday to coach her son's baseball team. Celebrate work anniversaries in the company newsletter along with highlighting the % of employees who used their PTO and who stayed committed to their efforts to keep their work email shut down over the weekend. I spent four months in 2022 working with a 100-member team from an employee benefits company. One of their departments collectively set a team goal to take true lunch breaks at least twice a week. During this lunch break, they would aim to leave their desks and the building for at least thirty minutes to an hour of screen-free and work-free break. The team used a shared spreadsheet to track their breaks each week, and they gave one another permission to check-in if a team member had been seen at their desk for two or three days in a row during lunch. Talk about positive accountability and healthy metrics! It should not be surprising to know that the team reported increased levels of focus and higher productivity rates in the afternoons once they developed this new lunchtime habit.

- **Provide Well-Aligned Rewards and Recognitions**: In a culture of busyness, the promotions and praise go to the individuals who burn the midnight oil, wear more hats than any one head can truly handle, and have the outward appearance of being as "busy as a bee" no matter the time of day or day of the week. In a culture of contribution, leaders pull back the curtain to look beyond quantity to recognize and reward levels of quality. Employee reviews and evaluations are more heavily performance-based, not dominated by production numbers. Promotions are based on output and effort, and next-level titles include benefits and perks that encourage employee health and wellness, not simply a larger paycheck accompanied by more hours of hard work, hustle, and grind. Imagine the result of a law firm awarding partnership based on the number of lives their attorney's positively and significantly impacted, versus using the key metric of the ability to generate and sustain 100+ billable hours month after month, year after year. The number of attorneys knocking on the door and begging to work there would be immeasurable.

- **Build the culture with and for the team**: A culture of contribution cannot be created *for* the team. It is not simply a list of values that compliment the company's mission and vision statements. A culture of contribution, like any other culture, is created when each individual member of the team walks the talk, starting with the leaders. Hold structured and unstructured conversations frequently about culture, productivity, and contribution, with larger groups and in more personal one-to-one discussions. Use these meetings to discuss the most important qualities and criteria employees believe support a culture of contribution. It cannot be said often enough: **lead by example and walk the talk**. I have seen what happens over and over again when leaders take the "do as I say, not as I do" approach. Surprise, surprise: it fails every time. As a leader, be transparent and honest and have open communication about your own strategies implemented to create work-life balance. Build the culture **with** your employees, not **for** them.

Conclusion

The conversation around company culture is here to stay. Members of the younger generations are demanding it, and members of the older generations are beginning to feel more empowered to ask for and expect more from their company than simply a paycheck and health insurance benefits. Most of us in the workforce will spend 90,000 hours at work over a lifetime. That is 30% of our lifetime! Doesn't it seem logical, then, that organizations and leaders would be smart to invest in efforts to ensure that their people are in a place where they are happy, well supported, and are significant contributors to the mission and vision?

Creating a culture of contribution is beneficial for everyone – team members, leaders, and customers. It can also have a domino effect of positive impact on family members and the community at large.

What is one first step you can take this week or month, to begin creating a healthier culture of contribution in your workplace?

In the words of George Leonard:

"How to begin the journey? You need only to take the first step. When? There is always now."

Notes

1. Bellezza, Silvia, et al. "Research: Why Americans Are so
   Impressed by Busyness." Harvard Business Review, 26 Nov.
   2019, hbr.org/2016/12/research-why-americans-are-so-
   impressed-by-busyness.

Elisabeth Galperin

Elisabeth Galperin is a speaker, productivity coach, and sought-after trainer who is passionate about helping professionals perform at their peak & reach their potential in all facets of life. A recovering perfectionist, she works collaboratively with clients to improve personal habits, define & implement business systems, increase productivity & consistently perform at their peak – while avoiding burn-out and overcoming overwhelm. Her mission is to help clients feel in control of their lives, so they can achieve maximum productivity, profitability, and, most importantly, peace of mind.

As a keynote speaker, corporate trainer, and executive business coach, Elisabeth empowers professionals at all levels of their career to define productivity for themselves and provides accountability & partnership to her clients. Her relatability, accessibility and energy are unmatched.

Through the use of her signature system, The ASCEND Method™, Elisabeth teaches the fundamental, foundational systems and structures all professionals need for sustainable growth and success.

Connect with Elisabeth Galperin:

LinkedIn: https://www.linkedin.com/in/elisabethgalperin

Email: elisabeth@peakproductivitycoaching.com

Website: www.peakproductivitycoaching.com

12.

Curiosity at the Heart of Inclusion

The Heart of Shaping a Culture of Inclusion

Lina Clavijo | Customer Marketing Manager

I am sure the following scenario is not foreign to you.

You are at a large venue, whether it is a concert, a game, or for the theater. Intermission or halftime comes, and then you face the dreadful, interminable waiting line for the woman's bathroom. How many times have you calculated – talking from a woman's point of view here – when you should go to the bathroom to avoid the line? Thoughts circulate in your mind: "Will I miss my favorite song?" "Will I miss that gameplay I have been anticipating?" Have you cared to ask yourself, "Why is the line so disproportionally longer than the man's bathroom?" The most obvious response might be that women take longer while going to the bathroom. Bingo! Yes, that is part of the issue; but there are other aspects we don't think about so instinctively.

Women's bathrooms are not designed or planned to include women's varying needs. Furthermore, accessibility is often a challenge and in this world of gender fluidity, there are communities that might not even have an option when they need to use the facilities. Bathrooms are designed to comply with construction codes, budget demands, real estate restrictions, and – in most cases – designed and built by men. Don't misunderstand- I am not embarking upon a feminist rampage against men. I proudly identify myself as a feminist, but I believe in creating awareness to drive evolution, not pointing fingers and shaming others. I am just trying to illustrate inequality and exclusion with a real-life example that most of us could relate to. Going to the bathroom is a human need, and a bathroom's design and construction is a right-in-our-face example of not understanding the lived experiences and needs of others. This sounds dramatic, but think about it.

Outside of the bathroom, gender inequity continues to be a fact worldwide. Per the US Department of Labor Blog post of March 14, 2023, women working full time earn, on average, 83.7% of what men are paid for a full year's salary.[1] This inequity is even greater for Black and Hispanic women. Women represent nearly half the world's population, yet as of the 2022 World Economic Forum Global Gender Gap Report, women in leadership positions only account for 31% worldwide.[2] According to the report, gender parity is not advancing at impressive levels, and it will take another 132 years to close the global gender gap. For North America, the projection is less discouraging; at the current rate of progress, it will take us from sixty-two to fifty-nine years to close the gap.

Unfortunately, women are not the only group that is undervalued or underrepresented in the workplace. We also have to recognize other groups in terms of ethnic and racial identities, sexual orientation, and age, to name a few. All of these aspects of diversity impact someone's identity as well as their life/work experience. In the past decade or so, the spotlight has shifted to Diversity, Equity, and Inclusion in many sectors. Some of the spotlight comes because of changes within our society, generational transitions, and enforcement of anti-discrimination policies Also, organizations have started to understand that DE&I efforts are not a "nice to have" but a necessity with impactful and positive business implications. Many organizations are now including DE&I as part of their strategies for growth and culture transformation. However, there is still a lot of work to do in changing the mindset of considering DE&I initiatives as a "fix" for specific diversity KPI deliverables. As part of my research for this chapter, I read through research conducted by consulting firms such as The Boston Consulting Group and McKinsey & Company. Often, findings from these studies associate DE&I as a strong force to drive innovation, make companies more attractive and more resilient, increase retention, and reduce attrition ("Diversity at Work," BCG article, July 2017, and "How Diverse Leadership Teams Boost Innovation," BCG article, January 2018.)[3]

Organizations, regardless of their size, should adopt DE&I as a pillar for growth and evolution. The road ahead of us is still full of opportunities. There are a few definitions of DE&I out there.

The way I have come to understand it is as follows:

- Diversity is a fact; you have it or don't, and that can be your starting point.
- Equity is an educated choice of decisions
- Inclusion is a crafted choice of actions.

Diversity is definitely the first step, but without inclusion, it will not move us forward in the journey of transforming culture and providing platforms for underrepresented communities to thrive.

Inclusion is tricky. You never know what would make an individual feel included or excluded. I bet we all have felt excluded at some point in our lives. I know I have. Growing up, I moved around my country as my father progressed in his career. I was the new student at school many times and faced the terror of not being accepted and having to make new friends. In my adult life, I have moved to different cities, countries, and continents many times and often experienced a feeling that I didn't belong. I was never aware of the difference between fitting in and belonging. Recently, I found a definition by Brene Brown: "Fitting in is becoming who you think you need to be accepted. Belonging is being your authentic self and knowing that no matter what happens, you belong to you."[4] That made me ask myself where I wanted to be:

Do I want to fit in? Or do I want to belong?

I realized that belonging gave me the space to be myself- to be who I am, unapologetically, authentically, and happier. At work, we all crave that feeling of belonging. We spend so many hours in our life at our offices, or doing our jobs, that we can't afford to be miserable. We must transform our corporate culture and create an environment where people feel valued, and empowered, and, therefore, more productive. We thrive when we are happy at work and feel that we belong. That is the culture I feel compelled to work in and to help build.

At the beginning of 2023, the company I work for launched a series of DE&I initiatives, including one called Courageous Conversations, to raise DE&I awareness and reinforce an inclusive culture. I had the opportunity to apply for a Facilitator role. It was a short application that included a brief video in which I needed to explain why this was important to me and what I expected to get out of the experience. Facilitating Courageous Conversations is outside my area of responsibility and scope of work as a Customer Marketing Manager for North America. I couldn't resist the urge to step in and try something new and jumped at the opportunity, even if it meant facing some time management challenges. I felt compelled to be part of this as I saw a great opportunity to contribute to something good for me and the collective well-being. This experience was full of surprises for me but, above all, very enriching. I have always felt that diversity is part of who I am. Per my definition above, diversity is a fact. We are all diverse in some way. I am an immigrant. I have lived in South America, the Caribbean, Europe, and North America and have been exposed to many different cultures. I have learned through those experiences how impactful it is to share and celebrate our differences and learn from each other. I am a strong LGBTQ+ community ally as my daughter is bisexual, and some of my closest friends are also part of this community. Still, I have come to realize how much more I must learn about diversity and the challenges every community faces. As part of the training to become a facilitator, I had to take the Harvard Implicit Association Test (IAT).[5] This test is designed to help you understand the strength of the association between concepts and evaluations or stereotypes that are stored at an unconscious level in your mind.We all have unconscious bias and it doesn't mean we are a bad person it only means we are human. We make assumptions based on our context and experiences. The value of understanding our own bias comes from realizing when unconscious bias is blinding us. Before taking the test, I felt confident that my level of implicit bias was low, given my life experiences, values, and character. What a humbling experience taking this test was for me. Facing my own bias scared me; it made me think about how biased people with less exposure to diversity might be. At the same time, it sparked a great deal of curiosity and commitment to drive awareness and become a culture shaper and barrier breaker.

Through the training process, I learned concepts that helped me understand some of my own experiences and learn from other members of the facilitators' community. Learning to confidently identify microaggressions, the emotional tax they cause, and the behaviors they trigger is key in driving bias awareness and building allyship. Microaggressions happen in the workplace more often than not. In one of Catalyst(1) Knowledge Burs -Catalyst is a nonprofit organization that drives change with preeminent thought leadership, actionable solutions, and a galvanized community of multinational corporations to accelerate and advance women into leadership – I found the following definition:

> "Microaggression: An act that insults, dehumanizes, excludes, or undermines people from marginalized groups, stems from deep-rooted biases, and is perceived by the initiator as harmless, inconsequential, and ordinary."

I have personally experienced being the target of microaggressions; I have also witnessed people around me become targets of microaggressions, and yet I didn't fully understand the meaning. In most cases, I found myself short of words to respond. On many occasions, microaggressions and bias-based comments catch you by surprise, which is why sometimes we freeze. We may ask ourselves well after the fact: *Why didn't I answer this?* This is such a frustrating feeling, isn't it? If you Google "How to respond to microaggression?" you will find plenty of formulated suggestions. However, we can't formulate and memorize a script. My learning is not to assume the intention was bad. Let's assume that people are doing the best they can with what they have and leverage the power of curiosity. Ask simple questions to understand where the comment is coming from, and hopefully, that will trigger some introspection in the person making the comment.

As part of the Courageous Conversations, we use examples of microaggressions or work scenarios of exclusion or bias to prompt the dialogue. The conversation is kicked off by establishing ground rules and intentions. It is important to create an environment of psychological safety and respect so people feel comfortable sharing experiences or thoughts that might be uncomfortable. It is also important to discuss why the subject we are about to discuss is important. Sharing some facts about how certain marginalized groups experience inequality or bias is vital. Then, we break large groups into smaller ones and ask them to discuss their feelings about the example. Is this something that they have experienced or have seen happening in the workplace? How would they approach the situation, and what kind of actions they can take to mitigate bias and create a more inclusive culture? Here is where the magic begins. Starting the conversation is not always easy. It takes a while for people to start feeling comfortable with the uncomfortable. It is important to note that it only takes one person to start sharing.

As a facilitator, I have discovered that my most powerful tools are courage, curiosity, and CAREfrontation (a play on the word: confrontation). As facilitators, we are not there to persuade people or reach a consensus; our purpose is to engage participants in meaningful discussions around difficult topics and learn from each other. There is significant value in active listening to be able to ask thought-provoking questions that help raise mindfulness on biases. There is also tremendous value to be found in being authentic and vulnerable. Participants need a trusting environment, and both authenticity and vulnerability build trust. When I introduce myself as the Facilitator, I avoid using my work title; I show a picture with my name underneath and share a little bit about myself as a human. I describe who I am and what being a facilitator and part of this culture-shaping conversation means to me, both on a personal and professional level. Avoiding any title and just presenting my name helps me level the playing field and set the tone that these are human conversations facilitated by a human. Being vulnerable and sharing some of my life experiences has also helped break uncomfortable silences. I am mindful to keep it short and simple just enough to trigger an interaction.

For the first year, all the topics for these Courageous Conversations have been selected based on the UN's global calendar. The best way that we can honor marginalized communities is to act on their day of commemoration and talk about how we can become a more inclusive culture.

Courageous Conversation is an ongoing process; we need to expect and accept non-closure and help the participants understand this as well. We will not fix the world in a one-hour conversation, but keeping a good cadence and active conversations will certainly help transform the culture. There is a well of insights generated in these conversations that makes it crucial for all levels of leadership to take part. Not only will this help them become better leaders, but it will also help them make better decisions when it comes to inclusion initiatives. The ultimate value of having these conversations is the power to build communities and transform culture. We have had instances where several individuals feel that the topic is relevant to them, and other times we have had participants with whom the scenario doesn't resonate at all. In both cases, engaging in these talks is still extremely beneficial. You provide a platform for someone from an underrepresented community to speak up and be listened to and for others with different life experiences to become acquainted with the challenges some people face due to bias in the workplace and in life.

Seating in one of the Courageous Conversations tables is not the only place where leaders in an organization can help shape a culture of inclusion. The Boston Consulting Group developed the BLISS (Bias-Free, Leadership, Inclusion, Safety, and Support) Index.[6] This comprehensive, statistically rigorous tool uses modeling techniques to identify the feelings of inclusion that matter in the workplace. The results from the survey conducted in the summer and fall of 2022, drawing data from 27,000 employees and sixteen countries, including the US, showed that when employees feel that DEI initiatives are a priority for the organization's leaders, the levels of employee satisfaction significantly increase. For example: in companies where senior leaders demonstrate commitment to DE&I, 84% of employees feel valued and respected, and in organizations where leaders are not regarded as committed to DE&I, only 44% do. The importance of communicating leadership's commitment to DE&I cannot be overstated; however, it is also important to note that it can result in mistrust of leadership, employee dissatisfaction, and employee turnover.

"Our lives begin to end the day we become silent about things that matter." – Martin Luther King, Jr.

Initiatives such as Courageous Conversations, when done openly, authentically, and honestly, provide a safe space for people to speak up whether they are part of an unrepresented community or not. Active listening is also at the core of these conversations in order to drive bias awareness, explore taboo topics, identify non-inclusive behaviors and unlearn "old truths". Learning about each other's life experiences helps shape a culture of respect, appreciation and inclusion. Wherever you are in your DE&I journey as an individual or an organization, have the courage to be curious, CAREfront, and drive action.

Notes

1. Wendy Chun-Hoon, 5 Fast Facts: The Gender Wage Gap, US Department of Labor Blog, March 14, 2023. https://blog.dol.gov/2023/03/14/5-fast-facts-the-gender-wage-gap

2. Global Gender Gap Report 2022, World Economic Forum. Chapter 2.4 Gender gaps in leadership, by industry and cohort. July 13, 2022. https://www.weforum.org/reports/global-gender-gap-report-2022/in-full/2-gender-gaps-in-the-workforce-an-emerging-crisis?_gl=1*6sdc54*_up*MQ..&gclid=CjwKCAjwgqejBhBAEiwAuWHioPTDaQORudAq5gl_Wm5wzFaN0SzP9WMVmuovWtG3iW6uAsxrzs2xoBoCDlYQAvD_BwE#2-gender-gaps-in-the-workforce-an-emerging-crisis

3. Miki Tsusaka, Martin Reeves, Stephanie Hurder, and Johann D. Harnoss, Diversity at Work, July 2017. https://www.bcg.com/publications/2017/diversity-at-work Rocío Lorenzo, Nicole Voigt, Miki Tsusaka, Matt Krentz, and Katie Abouzahr, How Diverse Leadership Teams Boost Innovation, January 2018. https://www.bcg.com/publications/2018/how-diverse-leadership-teams-boost-innovation

4. Brenee Brown, YouTube, February 4,2022. https://youtu.be/CkC6PeseGds

5. https://implicit.harvard.edu/implicit/iatdetails.html

6. Novacek, Gabrielle, et al. "Inclusion Isn't Just Nice. It's Necessary." BCG Global, 2 Mar. 2023, www.bcg.com/publications/2023/how-to-improve-inclusion-in-the-workplace.

Lina Clavijo

Lina is global citizen, marketer, and author. She was born and raised in Colombia South America and has lived in different cities in the United States, the Caribbean and Europe. Lina leverages her powerful storytelling skills in both her work as global brand marketer and in her most recent work as an author.

Diversity, Equity and Inclusion work has become one of Lina's strongest passions, she has embarked in the journey of learning how to contribute to corporate culture shaping and help underrepresented communities speak up and be heard. As a Courageous Conversations facilitator Lina has become a strong voice and role model for women in the organization she works for and is active contributor to advancing DEI efforts as a council member. Having lived in South America, the Caribbean, Europe and now North America, change is nothing new to Lina. Her learned experiences have given her a chance to celebrate differences in others. As an immigrant, she understands how enriching and necessary it is to share and learn from one another.

Lina is the proud mother of two, loves exploring the city, considers herself a 'foodie', travels and enjoys educating others on spiritual growth. She loves the food culture of the city as well as cooking and entertaining family and friends. In addition, Lina belongs to a community of multi-cultural women who work in energy healing and spiritual growth. In her book The Christmas Cactus, she explores storytelling as a channel for ancestral healing in an honest account of her life experiences.

Lina has over 20 years of experience working as a marketing executive for global brands. She has worked for The Clorox Company, Johnson & Johnson, NicePak and Univision. She currently resides in Philadelphia working as Customer Marketing Manager for North America at Essity. Lina holds a BS in Communication and Advertising from Universidad del Sagrado Corazon and an MS in Corporate Communication and PR from NYU.

Connect with Lina Clavijo:

LinkedIn: https://www.linkedin.com/in/linamclavijo/

Email: 08lmcc@gmail.com

Conclusion

Thank you for supporting the authors of Culture Impact: Strategies to Create World-changing Workplaces. This book aims to help leaders of small-to-midsize companies with the tools and knowledge needed to create a workplace culture that inspires employees, drives innovation, and helps achieve organization's goals. These twelve authors have provided their expertise so that they can influence how to move culture to the forefront of a company or organizations thought processes and procedures to ensure each company's/organization's culture is world-changing.

There were several themes that emerged from the collaboration of authors in Culture Impact.

Some critical concepts included:

- Take the first step towards becoming an award-winning workplace and revolutionize your recruitment and retention strategies by applying for workplace awards, strengthening employee engagement, aligning initiatives to strategic goals, empowering employees, making a positive impact on customers, and earning the well-deserved recognition for your outstanding workplace culture.
- Actively engage in Courageous Conversations and

commit to creating an inclusive culture where everyone feels valued and respected.

- Transform your leadership style and creating a positive organizational culture by delving into inner critic work.
- Build impactful relationships and driving a positive culture by gaining self-awareness, understanding your team members, and aligning with your organization's values, mission, and culture.
- Align your brand perception and company culture by starting with purpose, creating specific and meaningful values, and authentically living those values in every action and decision.

We hope you, too, found a few good takeaways to implement within your organization.

At the end of each chapter, you can access each author's bio and contact information. Please connect with them directly. The authors are excited to connect and help you achieve your company's culture goals.

As a bonus – Culture Impact: Strategies to Create World-changing Workplaces is part of INM's next book series entitled "Business Impact." If you'd enjoyed learning more from our impressive collection of authors, we urge you to check out our other titles in the series.

- Talent Impact
- Forward Impact

Do you have a chapter inside you? Learn more on how to become an author with Influence Network Media at https://overnightauthor.com. We can help you amplify your voice and highlight you as the expert that you are!

If you already have a book, we'd love to support you in taking it to the next level as a speaker, training, podcaster or more! Check out https://inmauthor.com/influencer.

There are several ways to show appreciation to the authors and Influence Network Media. Please leave an honest review on the site you purchased your book. Or you can provide a review on LinkedIn, Facebook, or Google. We greatly appreciate your honest feedback and any time you can give to offer your thoughts.

Everyone has a story to tell, and everyone's voice deserves to be heard. Cheers to creating new chapters in books and life!

Jodi Brandstetter, CEO, Influence Network Media

About the Publisher:

We provide publishing & promotional services to business experts who want to become authors.

A media company that provides publishing and promotional coaching and services to authors who write non-fiction books around people in business. Founded by Jodi Brandstetter and Melanie Booher, Influence Network Media is a one-stop-shop to ensure your book is a bestseller and authors are able to use their book as a vessel to their career success.

Our offerings include:

- **Collective Book** Opportunities where you only need one chapter, bio and headshot to become an Amazon Best Selling Author!
- **Solo Bundle** Opportunities for Business Experts who want to write a book that becomes a course and presentation all in one.
- **Author2Influencer** courses focused on creating your media and speaking presence.

To learn more:
https://overnightauthor.com
Publishing@overnightauthor.com

Book Smarts Business Podcast

Short on time but big on growth? Then the Book Smarts Business Podcast is the podcast for you – the experienced, business professional who loves to listen to podcasts and read business books all in an effort to learn more about his/her profession, become an expert in their field, or maybe even become an entrepreneur down the road!

In 15 minutes, you will learn more about the expert authors, gain amazing insights and knowledge from their unique expertise, as well as the ins & outs about their book, and why they decided to write their book!

For a potential author, Book Smarts Business Podcast provides an avenue for business authors to showcase their expertise and book, and gain more readers for their book!

https://booksmartsbusiness.buzzsprout.com/